Sermons I Like to Preach

Alton E. Loveless

ISBN Soft cover 978-1-940609-29-4

This book was printed in the United States of America.

To order additional copies of this book, contact:

FWB Publications
1006 Rayme Drive
Columbus, Ohio 43207
Alton.loveless@prodigy.net
Or
www.amazon.com

FWB

Introduction

For 65 years I have been preaching the gospel of the Lord Jesus Christ. In the beginning days my sermons where short and to the point because I knew very little about the Bible at that time. As I learned they were longer and to the point!

When I attended Hendrix College, a United Methodist college, Dr. James Upton who was not only my mentor but professor in my Pulpit Speaking and Homiletic classes taught me how to manuscript sermons. This was probably one of the best things I ever did in sermon preparation. It helped me to organize the thoughts that God had directed me to in studying His word and in the presentation.

With time, my sermons were less manuscript and more built around an outline, chosen words that I wanted to emphasize, or in the alliteration of the message or the use of acrostics.

Contained in this book are representations of these various styles to those of you who have asked for my sermon outlines. I do hope you enjoy them as much as I have enjoyed preaching them.

Table of Contents

HOW DO YOU BUILD A GREAT CHURCH?

Acts 2:42-47

And they continued stedfastly in the *__apostles' doctrine__* *and fellowship, and in breaking of bread, and in prayers.*

[43] And fear came upon every soul: and many wonders and signs were done by the apostles.

[44] And all that believed were together, and had all things common;

[45] And sold their possessions and goods, and parted them to all men, as every man had need.

[46] And they, continuing daily with one accord in the temple, and breaking bread from house to house, did eat their meat with gladness and singleness of heart,

[47] Praising God, and having favour with all the people. And the Lord added to the church daily such as should be saved.

I. You build a great church with a great preacher

> You cannot be anything if you want to be everything. Solomon Schechter (1847-1915)
>
> There are countless words in the Bible for Leadership (18 etc)
>
> Luke 4:18
>
> The Spirit of the Lord is upon me, because he hath anointed me to preach the gospel to the poor; he hath sent me to heal the brokenhearted, to preach deliverance to the captives, and recovering of sight to the blind, to set at liberty them that are bruised,

A. Episkopos – Ephes. 4:11 And he gave some, apostles; and some, prophets; and some, evangelists; and some, pastors and teachers;
B. Presbuteros – 1 Tim. 3:1 This is a true saying, If a man desire the office of a bishop, he desireth a good work.
C. Poimen – Feeder of the flock - Acts 20:28 Take heed therefore unto yourselves, and to all the flock, over which the Holy Ghost hath made you overseers, to feed the church of God, which he hath purchased with his own blood.

II. YOU BUILD A GREAT CHURCH WITH A GREAT PEOPLE

Philip. 1:1 -- *Paul and Timotheus, the servants of Jesus Christ, to all the saints in Christ Jesus which are at Philippi, with the bishops and deacons:*

Romans 12:7 -- Or ministry, let us wait on our ministering: or he that teacheth, on teaching;

A. Diakonos ("To stir up the Dust")
B. Fellowship, relationship, discipleship, worship, followship
C. Determined – Heped up
Dedicated – Humbled
Dependable – Happy
Saved – Called out
Sanctified – Called in
Separated – Called up

O Lord, help us to be thankful that you have "not dealt with us after our sins; nor rewarded us according to our iniquities (Psa. 103:10).

This world is God's house. He's left clues everywhere about what kind of God he is.

- When you stand at the Grand Canyon, you can't help but be overwhelmed at the mighty power of God to create such magnificence. He must have had a mighty hand to scoop out the Royal Gorge in Colorado.
- He is as infinite as the dark recesses of the mighty Atlantic Ocean.
- Each snowflake testifies to his uniqueness.
- The changing colors of the Great Smoky Mountains proclaim his creativity.

The galaxies shout out, "He is there."

- The wildflowers sing together, "He is there."
- The rippling brooks join in, "He is there."
- The birds sing it, the lions roar it, the fish write it in the oceans—"He is there."

All creation joins to sing his praise.

- The heavens declare it, the earth repeats it and the wind whispers It—"He Is there."
- Deep cries out to deep,
- The mighty sequoia tells it to the eagle who soars overhead,
- The lamb and the wolf agree on this one thing—"He is there."

No one can miss the message. God has left his fingerprints all over this world. Truly, "This is my Father's world," and every rock, every twig, every river and every mountain bear his signature. He signed his name to everything he made. The earth is marked

"Made By God" in letters so big that no one fails to see it. *"The heavens declare the glory of God; the skies proclaim the work of his hands"* (Psalm 19:1).

To call him the Father Almighty means that we can trust him in every circumstance because he will do whatever needs to be done to take care of us.

Romans 8:31-32 expresses this truth beautifully: *"What, then, shall we say in response to this? If God is for us, who can be against us? He who did not spare his own Son, but gave him up for us all—how will he not also, along with him, graciously give us all things?"*

What is the limit of the "all things" in verse 32? Answer: There is no limit.

Whatever we truly need, our Father will make sure that we have it because he is the "Father Almighty." His name is El Shaddai—Almighty God.

III. YOU BUILD A GREAT CHURCH WITH A GREAT PASSION

A. "Look on the Fields...White unto Harvest.
- Motion without movement
- Vision without victory
- Religion without revival
- Spirituality without Salvation
- Doxology without Devotion
- Cause without Cure
- Sadness without Sight
- Prayer without Power
- Enthusiasm without Examination
- Profession without procession

B. After Pentecost they were translated to perform

- Experiences into Expeditions
- Cleansing into Campaigning
- Worship into work
- Communion into commission

C. 120,000,000 were in the Roman Empire at the time
120 disciples in the upper room...500 invited
But the Holy Spirit overwhelmed those that came. The odds were 1 million to one.

- Religious Bigotry in Jerusalem
- Materialism in Ephesus
- Military Might of Rome
- Idolatry of Athens
- Intellectualism of Greece
- Rationalism of Sadducees
- Ritualism of Pharisees

Half the known world was saved before Paul's death.

- Scaffolds became pulpits
- Coliseums became witness stands
- Sign of the Fish

The three foundational documents of the Christian church— THE TEN COMMANDMENTS, THE LORD'S PRAYER, AND THE APOSTLES' CREED.

THE APOSTLES' CREED
I believe in God, the Father Almighty,
the Creator of heaven and earth,
and in Jesus Christ, his only son, our Lord:
Who was conceived of the Holy Spirit,
born of the Virgin Mary,
suffered under Pontius Pilate,

was crucified, died, and was buried.
He descended into hell.
The third day he rose again from the dead.
He ascended into heaven
and sits at the right hand of the Father Almighty,
whence he shall come to judge the living and the dead.
I believe in the Holy Spirit,
the holy Christian church,
the communion of saints,
the forgiveness of sins,
the resurrection of the body,
and life everlasting.
Amen.

- The Creed reminds us that truth is not optional.
- There are boundaries to the Christian faith.
- Not everything is negotiable.
- Some things must be believed if you are to call yourself a Christian.
- You can choose to live outside those boundaries, but if you do, you aren't a Christian and you shouldn't call yourself one.

This leads us to a vital truth point: Christianity is a doctrinal faith. It is not an "X" that you can fill in with whatever content you desire.

Note that when the Creed calls God the "Maker of heaven and earth," it parts company with Hinduism and by extension, with all the Eastern religions.

When it declares that Jesus is the Christ, God's only Son, and our Lord, it parts company with Islam and Judaism. This claim for Jesus makes Christianity utterly unique.

These titles were commonly used by the early church to describe their faith. Sometimes they used the familiar symbol of the fish, which in Greek is IXTHUS. Those letters were an acrostic for four of the words found in this phrase of the Creed:

- The letter I is the first letter of "Jesus" in Greek.
- The letter X is the first letter of "Christ" in Greek.
- The letters TH stand for the first letter of "God" in Greek.
- The letter U is the first letter of "Son" in Greek.
- The letter S is the first letter of "Savior" in Greek.
- So the word IXTHUS (and the fish symbol) stood as shorthand for: Jesus Christ, God's Son, our Savior.

  What have we learned from the Scriptures?
  - Old Testament—Anticipation
  - Gospels—Incarnation
  - Acts—Proclamation
  - Epistles—Explanation
  - Revelation—Consummation

- The Old Testament says, "He is coming!"
- The Gospels say, "He is here!"
- The book of Acts says, "He has come!"
- The Epistles say, "He is Lord!"
- Revelation says, "He is coming again!"

IV. YOU BUILD A GREAT CHURCH WITH A GREAT PROGRAM

To quote Buddha, He once said that if one person conquers in battle a thousand times a thousand and another conquers himself, he who conquers himself is the greatest of all conquerors. But how much do we know about self-conquest, self-mastery, and self-control? Why do I say that love is balanced by self-control? Because love is self-giving, and self-giving and self-control are complementary, the one to the other. How can we give ourselves in love until we've learned to control ourselves? Our self has to be mastered before it can be offered in the service of others.

-- John Stott, "A Vision for Holiness," Preaching Today

A. M ethods
O bjective
D ependence
E nthusiasm
L ife

B. Revival..

- A revival breaks the power of the world and the sin over the Christian.
- Revival...Always begins a new beginning of obedience to God.

C. A Revival may be expected when:

1. The providence of God indicates a revival is at hand.
2. The wickedness of the wicked grieves and humbles and distresses the Christian.
3. When Christian have a spirit of prayer for Revival
4. When Christians begin to confess their sins one to another.
5. When every ones attention is directed toward revival.
6. When Christians are found willing to make sacrifice necessary to carry it on.
7. When Christians are willing to have God Promote it by what instrumentals He pleases.

My relationship with God is part of my relationship with men. Failure in one will cause failure with the other.

-- Andrew Murray in With Christ in the School of Prayer. Christianity Today, Vol. 35, no. 5.

D. Hindrances to Revival

1. A revival will cease when Christians become mechanical in the attempt to promote it.
2. A Revival will cease when Christians get the idea the work will go on without them.
3. A revival will cease when the Church prefers to attend to its own concerns rather that God's business
4. A revival will cease when Christians refuse to render to the Lord according to the benefits received.

PAUL BEING LET DOWN IN A BASKET

Acts. 9:19-25

I. **PERSECUTOR BECOME PREACHER**
A. STRAIGHTWAY HE PREACHED CHRIST (VS 20

II. **PREACHER BECOMES PERSECUTED**
VS.23-25 PAUL WENT ARABIA 3 years (Gal. 1:15-18)

WHO WAS PAUL?

TARSUS (BIRTHPLACE) rivaled Alexander & Athens as the educational center.

A. Born a Jew (Acts 22:3)
1. Tribe of Benjamin (Phil 3:5
2. Pharisee (son of a Pharisee (Acts 26:5,Acts 23:6
3. Father and Mother not named
4. Kinsmen (Sister Acts 23:16) others Romans 16:7-21

B. WENT TO JERUSALEM AT ABOUT AGE 13

1. Taught of Gamaliel (Acts 22:3 Beauty of the Law
2. Trained in strict Jew tradition but familiar with Greek Thought and Literature.

C. CONSENTED TO DEATH OF STEPHEN (Acts 8:1-3, Held garments Acts. 22:20

D. PERSECUTED TO THE DEATH THIS WAY (Acts 22:4

E. NEARLY SINGLE HANDEDLY BEGAN ONSLAUGHT ON THE EARLY CHRISTIAN CHURCH.

F. LETTERS OF AUTHORITY TO GO TO DAMACUS (ACTS 9
1. ANANIAS- Devout man according to law (Acts 22:2
2. House of Judas
3. Street called STRAIGHT
-A lane from east gate to west gate.
3 lanes lined with Corinthian pillars

WHO HELD THE ROPES?

1. Disciples (who were they? His converts?
2. Held ropes by night. . Until his job was done

THEY DID NOT KNOW WHO WAS IN THEIR BASKET

PAUL- HISTORY OF PAUL

1. They did not know he would write 14 of the 27 books of the N.T.

2. That he would preach to gentiles, kings, and be a missionary

To the world. A pastor to pastors.

3. Have a heart of stone toward Stephen but turned to love as to Philemon' slave Onesimus.

4. Would write Romans and Galatians which would have a profound effect on the world.

8% of Acts tell of Paul's conversion

2/3rd of Acts tell of Paul's story of the early church.

HOW HIGH WAS THE WALL OF DAMASUS?

HERODITUS, THE GREEK HISTORIAN RECORDS:

- The city was 56 miles around
- The city was 14 miles on all 4 sides
- The city was 311 feet high
- The city was 87 feet thick at the top
- The city had 25 gates on each side (100 in all) 75 feet high that opened into roads 350 feet wide that went completely across
- the city to the other gate.
- The city had home 2-3 stories high
- The city had a moat that ran completely around the outer wall.
- The city contained the hanging gardens that when 400 into the air. The gardens were built by Nebuchadnezzar for his median queen wife and it perfumed the whole city.

A ROWDY TO A RECUITER
A RECUITER TO A REVIVALIST

WHO IS IN HIS BASKET?

1. Who was Edward Kimbell?
2. There was a young man, Who was born Feb. 5, 1837
3. He was one of 9 children
4. He was baptized by a Unitarian, the Rev. Oliver Everett at age 6.
5. He moved to Boston at age 17.
6. His uncle, Samuel Holton offered him a job on these terms.
    a. Approve the place the boy would live.
    b. Not go out at night to questionable places.
    c. Regularly attend the Mt. Vernon Church

EDWARD KIMBELL TAUGHT FRESHMAN STUDENTS FROM HARVARD IN THE MT. VERNON CONGREGATIONAL CHURCH.

1. Kimbell went of Visitation and led this Young man to the Lord on April 21, 1855.

2. He united with the Mt. Vernon church on May 1855

3. His testimonies kept him in trouble at the church because DR. Kirk was not getting to preach much of the time.

MOST HAVE NEVER HEARD OF EDWARD KIMBELL BUT MOST HAVE HEARD OF DWIGHT L. MOODY WHO HE LED TO CHRIST.

D.L. MOODY MOVED TO CHICAGO IN SEPT. 1856 AT AGE 19.

1. Joined Plymouth Congregational church.

2. Commenced immediately to work.

3. Rented 4 pews in the church which he fills immediately

4. He was never ordained to preach by a local church or denomination.

5. He soon gave away all the tracts and bibles from that church and joins First Methodist in Chicago.

6. He started a Sunday school on the North side. His told the numbers from the influential they could teach if they brought their own students.

SOON MEETS A PRESBYTERIAN ELDER NAMED J.B. STILLSON

1. Moody and Stillson had started 20 Sunday schools before he completes his 20th birthday.

2. At 21 he rented a deserted saloon and before long was averaging 600 and at times had as many as 1500 in 80 classes taught by volunteers.

3. At 23 he quit his job to devote full time to Christian work. He vowed to witness to someone about Christ each day.

4. At 24 He was president of the YMCA and his zeal had him ministering to 300,000 Union solders having conduced 1500 services for them.

5. At 26 he built the Illinois Ave. Church

6. Before Moody dies he had preached to ore that 100 million people. He died in 1892

7. He had heard Evangelist Haley in England whose words challenged him. The Evangelist misquoted John Knox but the meaning was still left in his following message: "It yet remains to be seen what one man will do that is totally committed to him." THE WORDS OF KNOX WAS: "The world has yet to see what god will do with, and for, and through, and in, and by, the man who is fully consecrated to him."

8. D.L. Moody preached later in England and F.B. Meyer heard him. Meyer preaches in the U.S. and Wilbur B. Chapman is challenged. Chapman challenges Billy Sunday, Moriciah Hamm then challenges Billy Graham.

CONCLUSION: SEE something
SET OUT to do it.
SELECT someone to help you.
SATUATE WITH PRAYER.

MASS EVANGELISM AS WE KNOW IT TODAY HAS IT ROOTS IN A SUNDAY SCHOOL TEACHER NAME EDWARD KIMBELL.

HEAVEN

Job 14:14, *"If a man die, shall he live again?"*

Pharaohs-Pyramids

Babylonians and Assyrians – Road signs in Heaven. They believed a large cavern exists.

Greek philosophers- Socrates and Plato argued for the indestructibility of the soul.

Aztecs-Toltecs-Incas records a belief in a hereafter.

HEAVEN IS REAL:

Designed by god:

1 COR. 2:9 But *as it is written, Eye hath not seen, nor ear heard, neither have entered into the heart of man, the things which God hath prepared for them that love him.*

Job 19:25 *For I know that my redeemer liveth, and that he shall stand at the latter day upon the earth: 26 And though after my skin worms destroy this body, yet in my flesh shall I see God: 27 Whom I shall see for myself, and mine eyes shall behold, and not another; though my reins be consumed within me.*

Declared By Jesus

John 11:25 *Jesus said unto her, I am the resurrection, and the life: he that believeth in me, though he were dead, yet shall he live:*

John 14: 19 *Yet a little while, and the world seeth me no more; but ye see me: because I live, ye shall live also.*

John 14: 14:1 *Let not your heart be troubled: ye believe in God, believe also in me.*

2 *In my Father's house are many mansions: if it were not so, I would have told you. I go to prepare a place for you.*

3 And if I go and prepare a place for you, I will come again, and receive you unto myself; that where I am, there ye may be also.

4 And whither I go ye know, and the way ye know.

5 Thomas saith unto him, Lord, we know not whither thou goest; and how can we know the way?

6 Jesus saith unto him, I am the way, the truth, and the life: no man cometh unto the Father, but by me.

Developed by the bible: 481 times it speaks of heaven.

Described By John

Rev. 4:1 *After this I looked, and, behold, a door was opened in heaven: and the first voice which I heard was as it were of a trumpet talking with me; which said, Come up hither, and I will show thee things which must be hereafter.*

2 And immediately I was in the spirit; and, behold, a throne was set in heaven, and one sat on the throne.

3 And he that sat was to look upon like a jasper and a sardine stone: and there was a rainbow round about the throne, in sight like unto an emerald.

4 And round about the throne were four and twenty seats: and upon the seats I saw four and twenty elders sitting, clothed in white raiment; and they had on their heads crowns of gold.

Rev. 21:1 *And I saw a new heaven and a new earth: for the first heaven and the first earth were passed away; and there was no more sea.*

2 And I John saw the holy city, new Jerusalem, coming down from God out of heaven, prepared as a bride adorned for her husband.

3 And I heard a great voice out of heaven saying, Behold, the tabernacle of God is with men, and he will dwell with them, and they shall be his people, and God himself shall be with them, and be their God.

Delight Of My Soul

1 Cor. 15:55 *O death, where is thy sting? O grave, where is thy victory?*

1 Cor. 15:57 *But thanks be to God, which giveth us the victory through our Lord Jesus Christ. 58 Therefore, my beloved brethren, be ye steadfast, unmovable, always abounding in the work of the Lord, forasmuch as ye know that your labour is not in vain in the Lord.*

REAL PLACE:

I Kings 8:30 *And hearken thou to the supplication of thy servant, and of thy people Israel, when they shall pray toward this place: and hear thou in heaven thy dwelling place: and when thou hearest, forgive.*

Matt.6: 9 *After this manner therefore pray ye: Our Father which art in heaven, Hallowed be thy name.*

Phil. 3:20 *For our (citizenship) conversation is in heaven; from whence also we look for the Saviour, the Lord Jesus Christ:*

21 Who shall change our vile body, that it may be fashioned like unto his glorious body, according to the working whereby he is able even to subdue all things unto himself.

2 Cor. 5:1 For we know that if our earthly house of this tabernacle were dissolved, we have a building of God, a house not made with hands, eternal in the heavens.

HEAVEN IS READY:

2 Cor. 5: 8 We *are confident, I say, and willing rather to be absent from the body, and to be present with the Lord.*

HEAVEN IS RIGHT:

HEAVEN IS RESTORATION:

Rev. 21: 4 *And God shall wipe away all tears from their eyes; and there shall be no more death, neither sorrow, nor crying, neither shall there be any more pain: for the former things are passed away.*

5 And he that sat upon the throne said, Behold, I make all things new. And he said unto me, Write: for these words are true and faithful.

6 And he said unto me, It is done. I am Alpha and Omega, the beginning and the end. I will give unto him that is athirst of the fountain of the water of life freely.

7.He that overcometh shall inherit all things; and I will be his God, and he shall be my son.

Rev. 22: 3 *And there shall be no more curse: but the throne of God and of the Lamb shall be in it; and his servants shall serve him:*

4 And they shall see his face; and his name shall be in their foreheads.

5 And there shall be no night there; and they need no candle, neither light of the sun; for the Lord God giveth them light: and they shall reign for ever and ever.

HEAVEN IS REWARD:

Rev. *21:24 And the nations of them which are saved shall walk in the light of it: and the kings of the earth do bring their glory and honour into it.*

25 And the gates of it shall not be shut at all by day: for there shall be no night there.

26 And they shall bring the glory and honour of the nations into it.

Rev. 22:12 *And, behold, I come quickly; and my reward is with me, to give every man according as his work shall be.*

HEAVEN IS REUNION: Our son, our parents, our friends

HEAVEN IS RESTRICTED:

Rev. 20: 11 *And I saw a great white throne, and him that sat on it, from whose face the earth and the heaven fled away; and there was found no place for them.*

12 And I saw the dead, small and great, stand before God; and the books were opened: and another book was opened, which is the book of life: and the dead were judged out of those things which were written in the books, according to their works.

13 And the sea gave up the dead which were in it; and death and hell delivered up the dead which were in them: and they were judged every man according to their works.

Rev. 21:8 But *the fearful, and unbelieving, and the abominable, and murderers, and whoremongers, and sorcerers, and idolaters, and all liars, shall have their part in the lake which burneth with fire and brimstone: which is the second death.*

Rev. 21: 27 *And there shall in no wise enter into it anything that defileth, neither whatsoever worketh abomination, or maketh a lie: but they which are written in the Lamb's book of life.*

Rev. 22: 15 For *without are dogs, and sorcerers, and whoremongers, and murderers, and idolaters, and whosoever loveth and maketh a lie.*

John Jasper – served God in excitement

Arnold Pollard- Believe God in trouble

Pastor Ki- Sold out to God when no one seemed to care but God.

CHARLEY MC COY...AT AGE 72 was given keys to Florlda

Died at age 88 in India.

Famous Soong Sisters

THE LORD IS MY SHEPHERD; I SHALL NOT WANT

This is the John 10 of the O.T., with the sheep experiencing the more abundant life provided for them by the Messiah

(Psalm 23:1-6; John 10:1-18).

Thirty Perfect Things of Psalm 23

1. The Lord—perfect God (Psalm 23:1)
2.My Shepherd—perfect Keeper
3.Not want—perfect satisfaction
4.Maketh me—perfect Director (Psalm 23:2)
5.Lie down—perfect rest
6.Green pastures—perfect supply
7.Leadeth me—perfect guidance (Psalm 23:2-3)
8.Still waters—perfect peace
9.Restoreth—perfect restoration (Psalm 23:3)
10.My soul—perfect self
11.Paths of righteousness—perfect holiness (Psalm 23:3; Hebrews 12:14)
12.Name's sake—perfect object
13.Though I walk through the valley of the shadow of death—perfect trust (Psalm 23:4)
14.Fear no evil—perfect protection
15.With me—perfect companionship
16.Thy rod—perfect defense
17.Thy staff—perfect help
18.Comfort me—perfect solace
19. Preparest—perfect provision (Psalm 23:5)

20.Table—perfect food
21.Before me—perfect presence
22.In presence of enemies—perfect safety
23.Anointest my head with oil—perfect anointing
24.Cup runneth over—perfect joy
25.Surely—perfect assurance (Psalm 23:6)
26.Goodness—perfect benevolence
27.Mercy—perfect compassion
28.Follow all my days—perfect life
29.Dwell—perfect home
30.In the house of the Lord forever—perfect destiny

The LORD

IS---exists

MY--possessive. He is mine.

God is called the Shepherd of Israel (Genesis 49:24; Psalm 80:1; Isaiah 40:9-11). He predicts setting over them one shepherd who will be true to Israel (Ezekiel 34:23; Ezekiel 37:24; Zech. 13:7; Matthew 26:31).

How can we keep our sanity when the world is turning upside down? How can we, as Rudyard Kipling put it, "keep your head when all about you is losing theirs and blaming it on you." For centuries Jews and Christians have turned to Psalm 23 for guidance and encouragement.

We live in a world where storms blow and danger awaits around every turn. We live in a world of disease and death, of heartache and loneliness, and our only peace comes through the protective presence of our Lord Jesus Christ.

As the line from a poem goes: "When you cannot trace his hand, trust his heart."

The Lord is my shepherd, I shall not want.

Doesn't your breath, just ease a little when you hear those words? The Lord is my Shepherd. It's really quite a statement. The Lord is in charge. God directs me and cares for me. God looks for me when I am lost and rejoices when I am found. There is one in charge. And it is God.

ON THE NIGHT OF MY SECOND OPERATION AT 3 A.M. ONE OF THE NURSES WAS A BLACK LADY WHO I LOOKED UP TO AND SAID 'DO YOU PRAY FOR WHITE GENTLEMEN HEADED FOR SURGURY? SHE DID!!

"I shall not want" certainly expresses a confidence in God - to take care of the things. God will not leave me lacking.

But it also becomes a decision that I must make, a decision against greed and lust and hoarding. I shall NOT want. It isn't easy to not want, when our consumer society reminds us again and again to want, to desire, to buy, to get. But I can be free of that - The Lord is my Shepherd; I shall not want.

"He makes me lie down in green pastures and leads me beside still waters."

The very first thing that God encourages us to do, runs contrary to almost everything else in our society.

- God wants us to be still.
- Slow down.
- Lie down.

Listen to your own heartbeat for a while. God leads us beside still waters... sheep cannot drink from raging waters, there is no nourishment because they are afraid of the fast water. God slows things down so that we can be nourished.

"He restores my soul. He leads me in right paths for his name's sake."

Then comes, perhaps, the most famous line of the psalm - in the King James Version that most of us learned, it read:

"Yea, though I walk through the valley of the shadow of death, I will fear no evil, for thou art with me."

God knows all about our world. We all walk in the valley of the shadow of death sometimes.

> We can still feel utterly alone.
> But we are not alone: God is with us.

In that valley the psalmist says, "I will fear no evil, for you are with me!"

But more than the assurance that we are not alone, God also promises to help us get out of the valley. God offers us a table - food for our souls. God offers us oil - a balm for our wounded spirit. God offer us a cup - drink and refreshment for our lives.

"You prepare a table before me in the presence of my enemies; you anoint my head with oil; my cup overflows."

1. God will
    - feed us
    - Heal Us
    - Refresh us.

"You prepare a table before me in the presence of my enemies."

Finally, the psalm concludes with an affirmation - a celebration.

"Surely goodness and mercy shall follow me all the days of my life, and I shall dwell in the house of the LORD my whole life long."

But even as I journey, I will have a sense of always being at home in God's presence: I will dwell in the house of the Lord, forever.

The LORD is my shepherd; I shall not want.
(Psalm 23:1)

Before a shepherd can be fully considered - it is painfully obvious that someone is represented by the sheep.

A. Sheep have a great tendency to stray (Isa. 53:6; Ps. 119:176).

B. As a result of wondering, they become very vulnerable (Jer. 50:17) - Daniel (Lion & Bear) (1 Sam. 17:34). The Lion represents the Devil, and the Bear represents the enemies Greece and Russia.

C. Sheep require high maintenance - David a shepherd, needed a better one.

Why would you want the LORD to be your shepherd?

A. He knows his sheep (Jn. 10:14). How many important people that are in your life do not know you? - High School Principal, Elected Officials, Military Officers, etc.

B. He leads his sheep (Ps. 77:20; 78:52; 79:13; 80:1).

C. He leads his sheep to good pasture (vs. 2).

D. Defends them when attacked by wild beast (1 Sam. 17:34-36).

E. Searching them out when straying (Lk. 15:4-6).

F. Attending them when they are sick (Eze. 34:11-16).

G. Warns them of a false shepherd (Zech. 11:16-17).

"I Shall Not Want"

How many Americans can truly say "I shall not want"? We live in a land of want. Millions are in tremendous financial trouble, not because of needs, but because of wants.

I. Is it wrong to want?

How about a meal, reliable transportation, a job that can pay the bills, a good marriage, good children, good education, etc.

A. When the wants follow the right priority list.

[1]. Spiritual (Matt. 6:33)

But if thine eye be evil, thy whole body shall be full of darkness. If therefore the light that is in thee be darkness, how great is that darkness!

[2]. Emotional (Mk. 12:30)

And thou shalt love the Lord thy God with all thy heart, and with all thy soul, and with all thy mind, and with all thy strength: this is the first commandment.

[3]. Physical (Phil. 4:19)

But my God shall supply all your need according to his riches in glory by Christ Jesus.

B. When my wants are accompanied by an acknowledgment that God is supplying them all (Phil. 4:11). The strictest interpretation of this verse would suggest that all discontentment is ultimately a criticism of God. Philip. 4:11

Not that I speak in respect of want: for I have learned, in whatsoever state I am, therewith to be content.

- When there is a spirit of contentment in the pasture that he has led you to - it is difficult for us to believe that pastures of adversity could be from God, not realizing the advantages of adversity.

God's Green Pastures (Psalm 23:2)

The Bible has much to say about Sheep, Shepherds, and Pastures - it was almost a universal language in Bible times.

I. Pasture of Salvation - (Jn. 10:1-9)

A. Sheepfold - high stone fence with one door.

B. Porter - hired night watchman - (slept in door way).

C. Voice - sheep respond to shepherd voice (vs. 27-30).

D. Saved - comes from acknowledging who the door is and by going through that door.

When Dr. Harry Ironside was guest of friends who raised sheep in Washington State, one morning he was startled to see an old ewe go across the road followed by the strangest looking lamb! It had 6 legs and the last 2 were hanging helplessly as if paralyzed, and skin seemed partly torn from its body.

One of the herders explained: "The lamb is really not the ewe's! The latter did have a lamb which was bitten by a rattlesnake and died. The ewe seemed remorseful, and refused to accept a new lamb which was an orphan and needed a mother. At first she sniffed at it and pushed it away, apparently saying: "That's not our family odor!"

So the herders skinned the dead lamb and carefully drew the fleece over the living lamb - leaving hind legs hanging loose. The ewe smelled it again and was satisfied and adopted it as her own.

II. Pastures of the Wilderness - (Ps. 65:9-13)

Natural inclination is to assume the wilderness is associated with desolation - but quite to the contrary. Mountain wilderness areas possess some of the best pasture (Isa. 49:8-11).

Wilderness pastures are a place that are:

A. Difficult to get to.
B. Isolation from the world.
C. Dependence upon God.
D. Great grass.

Lie down in green pastures –

Phillip Keller, once a shepherd himself, in his book *A Shepherd Looks at Psalm 23,* relates:

- *The strange thing about sheep is that because of their very makeup, it is almost impossible for them to be made to lie down, unless four requirements are met.*

  First, due to their timidity, they must be free from all fear.

  Next, because of their sociability, they must be free from friction with others of their kind.

  Third, they must be free from flies or parasites if they are to relax.

  Lastly, they will not lie down unless free from hunger.

  And it is only the shepherd who can provide release from all anxieties.

- Sheep need to have the right shepherd due to their own peculiarities.

Shepherds can water their sheep with other sheep but they always return to their shepherd.

III. Pastures of Ingratitude - (Hos. 13:4-9)

Wilderness pastures which ate green and rich often turn into drought because hearts are exalted and God is forgotten. (Joel 1:18-20) Never has America had so much and yet so little spiritual pasture.

A simple song of gratitude may save your life!

Ira D. Sankey was traveling by steamboat up the Delaware River. It was a calm, starlit evening and there were many passengers gathered on the deck. Mr. Sankey was asked to sing. Somehow he was driven to sing the hymn "Saviour, Like A Shepherd Leads Us."

"Can you remember when you were doing picket duty on a bright moonlight night in 1862?" asked a passenger.

"Yes," answered Mr. Sankey, very much surprised.

"So do I," said the stranger, "but I was serving in the Confederate Army. I saw you raised your eyes to heaven and began to sing. Music has always had a wonderful power over me, and I took my finger off the trigger.

"Let him sing his song to the end, I said to myself, I can shoot him afterwards." "but the song you sang then was the song

you just sang now. I heard the words perfectly: "We are Thine; do thou befriend us. be the guardian of our way."

"When you had finished your song, it was impossible for me to take aim at you again. I thought: "the Lord who is able to save that man from certain death must surely be great and might" - and my arm dropped limp by my side.

"Since that time I wandered about far and wide; but when I just now saw you standing there singing just as on that other occasion, I recognized you. Then my heart was wounded by your song. Now I wish that you may help find a cure for my sick soul."

Deeply moved, Mr. Sankey threw his arms about the man who had been his enemy. Then the stranger found Him who was their common Savior, the Good Shepherd.

IV. Pastures of Promise - (Joel 2:21-27)

Even though this is a millennial promise made to Israel in the future, we have overtones of Christian New Testament truth.

Example: (vs. 25) Paul says redeeming the time for the days are evil.

Shepherd Waits for Sheep's Surrender -

" In the highlands of Scotland, sheep would often wander off into the rocks and get into places that they couldn't get out of.

The grass on these mountains is very sweet and the sheep will jump down ten or twelve feet, and can't jump back again. They may be there for days, until they have eaten all the grass.

"The shepherd will wait until they are so faint that they cannot stand, and then he will put a rope around himself and go over and pull the sheep up out of the jaws of death. 'Why doesn't he go down there when the sheep first get there?' I asked. "'Ah!' he said, 'if they did, the sheep are so very foolish they would dash right over the precipice and be killed!'" - D.L. Moody

He Restoreth My Soul (Psalm 23:3)

The idea of restoration is taking something that's beat up, worn or rejected and making it useful - it brings a great sense of satisfaction.

What is a Soul?

A. It embraces the essence of life (Gen. 2:7).

B. Soul includes heart (emotions), mind (understanding), will (strength) (Mk. 12:33).

C. The soul goes on after death (Gen. 35:18-19). The Bible is clear that the soul gets used and abused so that it finds itself in regular need of restoration.

I. Malnutrition (weak) - (Ps. 107:5-9)

God's desire is to lead you to **green** pastures and still waters, but some soul starvation is a result of our own rebellion (Ps. 106:7-15). **Notice:** Having your request met, is not necessarily a healthy soul. This week was a time of soul feeding! (Ps. 107:8-9).

II. Wounded - (Job 24:12)

A. Bitterness - (Job 21:25; Eph. 4:31; Heb. 12:14-15)

B. Privation - (Ps. 109:21-22 - vs. 30, 31) Privation of friends, commodities, love, etc. exercise (Prov. 11:17).

III. Worn Out - (Matt. 11:28-30)
Burdened down with sin, doubt, guilt, unbelief, and a whole host of other things that the devil puts on a person in this life. Some however is self-induced.

IV. Wrong Soul - (Prov. 8:36)
Notice the sin is against wisdom - if any man lack wisdom, let him ask of God (Prov. 15:32-33).

A. Wrong soul is hell bound - (Prov. 23:13,14). This means the necessity of redemption (Ps. 49:15).

B. Scar Tissue - areas that have been injured and have not healed properly leave scar tissue. It is a sign of attack, battle, and sometimes... self-inflicted wounds.

V. The Won Soul - (Prov. 11:30)
A soul that has turned from darkness to light... from the path of unrighteousness to the path of righteousness and light through Jesus Christ.

The Valley Of The Shadow Of Death (Psalm 23:4)

A religion that does not prepare its adherents to die, is a shame. Some say, "all they want is your money" are correct --without death preparation.

I. It's an inevitable valley -
Princess Di - (Rom. 6:23; 7:24-25)

II. Evil is connected to it - (Heb. 2:14)

As negative as all this sounds, God has two items of comfort for us through the valley.

A. The Rod - A strong sapling with the roots whittled down to make a club - it could be thrown with amazing speed and accuracy.

[1]. A symbol of **Strength** and **Authority** (Ex. 4:1-5,17,20) - So the scriptures must be the **Rod**!

[2**]. Used to discipline** - If the shepherd saw the sheep wandering away, or approaching poisonous weeds, or getting too close to danger, the rod would go whistling thru the air to remind the sheep of the parameters. There is a great blessing knowing the boundaries (Exe. 20:33-38). Does not the Word discipline us?

[3]. **Used to examine us** - The skilled shepherd took his rod and parted the wool to look close to determine the condition of the skin etc. You cannot "pull the wool over His eyes" (Ps. 139:23,24) - The Word looks below the surface.

[4]. It is an instrument of protection both for himself and the sheep - The skilled shepherd uses his rod to drive off predators. After a life time of being under the protection of the book, it will comfort you in the valley.

B. The Staff - Is essentially a symbol of concern. Normally a long, slender stick, often with a crook or hook on one end. A picture of the Holy Spirit - do not go without it (Ex. 12:11).

[1]. Draws sheep together into an intimate relationship - The shepherd uses his staff to gently lift a newborn lamb and bring it to its mother without

leaving human scent and risking rejection. The Holy Spirit is intrinsically involved in the new birth process (Jn. 3:1-8).

[2]. **Used for guiding sheep** (Jud. 6:19-23 - confirmation) thru difficult terrain and passages. It is not an instrument to beat with, but to touch with and often used to stay in touch - after years of salvation sensing the touch of the Spirit - the valley of death will be one of shadows (Rom. 8:16).

[3]. **An instrument of rescue** - on steep cliffs, brambles, etc.

[4]. Connected with faith - (Heb. 11:21)

Death is the last enemy - (1 Cor. 15:25-26; Song Sol. 2:4)

What will not prepare you for death!

A. Prominence (Acts 26:27-28) - Becoming a Christian is the result of persuading (Acts 28:23-24), the more prominent, the more difficult it is to be persuaded. In the New Testament it was always the common people who responded.

B. Religion (Jn. 3) - notice what's missing in the equation - ceremony etc.

Birth implies:

[1]. A time experience
[2]. No past
[3]. A new beginning
[4]. A new name

C. Works (Eph. 2:8-9; Tit. 3:5-8)

- At Princess Di's funeral there was no sermon, only the briefest illusion to "Christ, who died for you." the emphasis was on works!

- Mother Theresa lived more righteous than most, I applaud her works, but it is not her works that need to be emulated to die with salvation. But for sake of conversation, let's say she is the standard - Jesus told the rich young ruler to sell what he had and give to the poor - have you done it?

You better be thankful it's "not of works".

-I was able to see my mother just hours before her death even though I had not seen her for 80 days. God had put us both in the hospital and I waved to her from my wheelchair when she was in ICU and I was preparing to return to Barnes Hospital in St. Louis.

Thou Anointest My Head With Oil (Psalm 23:5)

Have You Been Anointed?

Three occasions for anointing with oil - all three indicate God setting something aside for a special use.

I. **The Leper** - (Lev. 14:1,2,10-18)

A. Leprosy in the Bible is always a picture of the sinner in great need.
B. It is a spiritual problem as indicated by the victim being sent to the priest, not the physician.
C. The oil is poured on his head (vs. 18) as part of the atonement.
D. When you recognize Jesus Christ as your Shepherd, He anoints your leprosy and cleanses you! (2 Cor. 1:20-22)

II. The Priest - (Ex. 30:22-30), Leprosy dealt with - (Lev. 22:4)

A. As a child of God, you have been anointed to the priesthood - (1 Pet. 2:9).
B. Why? - to "shew forth the praises of him who hath called you out of darkness into his marvelous light."
C. We are recipients of God's mercy (vs. 10).
D. Act like a priest (vs. 11).

III. The King - (1 Sam. 16:1,13)
A. The king is the subject of the next chapter - (Ps. 24).
B. As a child of the King I am in line (Rom. 8:14-17; 2 Tim. 2:12).
C. Eventual kingship and all its entitlements come with salvation.
D. David was anointed King long before he became one.

IV. The Failure To Anoint Christ - (Lk. 7:36-50)
A. Is a failure to recognize him as the anointed one.
B. Failure to understand Christ's position in the father - (Ps. 45:6-7).

I Will Dwell In The House Of The Lord Forever (Psalm 23:6)

Review!

Did you ever wonder what some special house is like? Perhaps it was the biggest house in your town, or the most ornate, or the coziest in appearance or the one with the uncertain mystery! Have you ever given much thought to what God's house is like (Jn. 14:2)?

I. A picture of Heaven -

In the Old Testament, a house is a picture of Heaven (Heb. 9:19-24).

II. A Place of Peace - (Ps. 122)

Jerusalem is not presently a place of peace, but it will be someday. Heaven is! **NO CONFLICT**!

A. Peace **with** God - (Rom. 5:1); all your controversies with God will be over.
B. Peace **of** God - (Phil. 4:7); all your controversies with yourself - notice (vs. 8) has to do with what you think on!

III. A Place of Abiding Covenant - Eternal covenant (2 Kings 23:1, 2)

Christ is the mediator of a better covenant (Heb. 8:1-6)

"Forever, Oh LORD, Thy word is settled in heaven." (Ps. 119:89)

IV. A Place of Flourishing - (Ps. 92:12-15) not diminishing.

V. A Place of Beauty and Safety - (Ps. 27:4-14) easy on the mind! (Rev. 21:18-20)

VI. Payment of Vows - (Ps. 116:15-19) All guilt removed. You will follow thru with your vows.

MORE Than Conquerors

Romans 8

Romans Chapter 8. Read verse 37: "Nay, in all these things we are more than conquerors through him that loved us." This 8th chapter, as many of you know, begins a new section in this wonderful epistle to the Romans.

- The 7th chapter is a chapter of gloom and the
  - 8th chapter is a chapter of glory.
- The 7th chapter is a chapter of condemnation and the
  - 8th chapter is a chapter of emancipation.
- The 7th chapter is a funeral march and the
  - 8th chapter is a wedding march. It's the song of a "soul set free,"
- Romans 7 is a chapter on the tomb.
  - Romans 8 is a chapter on triumph.
- The 7th chapter is the chapter of paradise lost. It's a chapter of depravity.
  - The 8th chapter is a chapter of deliverance and delight.

Now this is a magnificent chapter. If you want to make a special bonding here,

- Chapter 7 is a chapter of misery and condemnation.

- The 8th chapter is a liberated soul.

You can explain this by this fact:

- Chapter 7 is a chapter on a self-centered person.
    - The 8th chapter is a chapter about the Christ-centered person.

In the 7th chapter you read that first person over and over and over until you get weary of reading "I, I, I, I,..." "I want to do this but I can't...," and "I find I'm in bondage...," and so forth and so on. If you count you'll discover 41 times you find that "I," and no mention of the Holy Spirit. In the 8th chapter there is no mention of the "I" except in two verses where he says "I reckon" and "I am persuaded" (where there is no alternative). But the difference in the 8th chapter is that there is all the mention in the world about the Holy Spirit. Nineteen times the Holy Spirit is mentioned.

Cardinal Hugo de Sancto Caro is often given credit for first dividing the Latin Vulgate into chapters and fellow cardinal Stephen Langton who in 1205 created the chapter divisions which are used today. Robert Estienne (Robert Stephanus) was the first to number the verses within each chapter, his verse numbers entering printed editions in 1551 (New Testament) and 1571 (Hebrew Bible)[15]

There is therefore now no condemnation..." So, the chapter begins away in the heights—there is no condemnation. And it ends—"there is no separation." "What shall separate us from the love of God?" But it does not say there is no tribulation. In fact, it marks tribulation out for us very, very carefully.

A wretched, sin-bound man in the 7th chapter and no Holy Spirit.

A liberated man in the 8th chapter, and over and over again he pays tribute to the Holy Spirit of God.

This is an amazing Word of God. Here is a man talking about emancipation. He's talking about an individual **having under his feet the world, the flesh, and the devil**. We'll get to it a bit later, but he says "In all these things..." and he doesn't leave you to fill in the blanks. He fills them in himself.

Nobody, I say, saw the depth of depravity Paul saw. He saw that because men had rejected the message of the Son of God, God gave them up to uncleanness.

Paul doesn't say how terrible the malady is. He's not concerned about the malady. ***He's concerned about the remedy!*** He said in Heb. 7:25, "He is able to save to the uttermost" and the "guttermost." Therefore, at the end of this amazing chapter he said,

"We are MORE than conquerors through Him that loved us."

The only reason there is an America tonight is, not because we signed the Declaration of Independence, but because **34 years before that time there was a revival that struck this country.**

Dr. Tozer, who once said, *"as soon as man got alienated from God, he got interested in things." Now I was reading through these chapters, and I noticed how many times Paul says that, "They that are after the flesh do mind the THINGS of the flesh, but they that are after the Spirit mind the THINGS of the Spirit."*

And then that very famous, popular verse: Romans 8:28. "All THINGS work together for good." Not some things. **All THINGS**.

- *Losses as well as gain;*
- *invisible things as well as visible;*
- *those that are bitter as well as those that are sweet*.
-

All things work together for good. I like to say the only way to read that verse is backwards. *"To them that love God, to them who are the called, according to His purpose, all things work together for good, To them that are called according to His purpose.* Now verse 31, "What shall we say to these THINGS? If God be for us, who can be against us?"

He says in verse 37, "Nay in all these THINGS..." You can almost hear his contempt there, can't you? "Things. So what?" And then he finishes the verse there in 38. I believe he throws his shoulders back and laughs in the face of the devil and says you haven't an invention in Hell that can separate me. That's what he says, doesn't he? Because he says here, at the end of verse 38, "I am persuaded." Are you persuaded tonight? Paul was a persuaded man. He was persuaded that God was able to keep that which he'd committed unto Him.

I'm persuaded tonight that neither height, nor depth, nor any other creature can separate me from the love of God. "For I'm persuaded that neither death, nor life, nor angels, nor principalities, nor THINGS present nor THINGS to come...!" If that isn't defiance I don't know what is.

One day, this man was going down the Damascus Road. Look! You know what? A man with an experience is never at the mercy of a man with an argument.

He was going down the Damascus Road, breathing out threatening. He carried documents that said he could put any Christian he liked to death. (It's exactly what the blundering, blind, bankrupt world that you and I live in did,) but he did not reckon with Jesus Christ Himself. And Jesus sits on His throne and met him in the road. Paul said, *"Who art thou? Lord?" "On that road,"* he said*, "He revealed Himself to me."* He said, "In the wilderness. In the school of silence." (It's still open if you want to go. It'll cost you nothing.) "On the Damascus Road God revealed Himself <u>to</u> me. There in the wilderness, He revealed Himself <u>in</u> me."

Then he soared up into heaven. I don't know all he saw except it was just so marvelous. The Lord said "Don't ever say a word about it. As long as you live, you can't tell anything you saw." And he never did!

- Sometimes I wonder if God rolled out the plans of the ages from the incarnation to the consummation.
- I wonder if he saw the day in which you and I live.
- I wonder if he saw the depravity that was going to strangle the world silent before Jesus comes.

There where he and God were alone, and God stripped him, what happened? I tell you; he became spiritually pregnant. He birthed these churches to whom he was writing here. He birthed these epistles in the Holy Ghost.

God put something in him that,

- When later he is put in the waters,
- Thirty-six hours in the Mediterranean; the waves couldn't wash it out.
- They lashed him one hundred ninety-five times; they couldn't whip it out.
- The devils chased him; they couldn't scare it out of him.
- They wouldn't give him any food; they couldn't starve it out of him.

You and I had better get an experience like that before long because the roof is going to come in before we go much further. God hasn't raised you up to be a bottle-fed baby from here to eternity. He's coming to gather His jewels out of your life. He's invested a lot in you. He didn't save you that you might escape eternal fire. That's a fringe benefit. He saved you that you might be conformed to the image of His Son, however costly that may be.

A lot of people say today when they talk about victorious life, "Well, you know what Paul said..." in the end of Romans chapter 7: *"Oh wretched man that I am!"* Well, I didn't need the Lord to tell me that. I know that well enough. But you see, we tack onto that another statement. We say—listen now to what the Scripture says: *"They that are in the flesh cannot please God."* But read the next verse: *"Ye are NOT in the flesh."* Now, what do you do with it? This flesh...Yes. But a fleshy nature, a lusting, sinful, greedy, lustful nature...No.

You see, Paul here uses one of the most amazing things in all his career. He says, *"Who shall deliver me from the body of this death?"* Now what will you do? Is that the end of the story? In the original there are no chapters. There's no 7th chapter and 8th chapter. The 7th goes right on into the 8th. Now what do you do? Do you stop at the end of Romans 7 and say Paul is saying all through his life, *"O wretched man that I am! I've another war raging in my members"?* What does he say? He says, "Who shall deliver me from the body of this death?" Well, tell me tonight, can Buddha do it? Can Confucius do it? Can transcendental meditation do it? No sir. A thousand times over. There is One who is able to do it.

You know, there were over **<u>120 different types of crosses</u>**.

- There was a traditional cross.
- There was a cross like the letter "T" on which a man's head was allowed to drop back.
- There was a cross like the letter "X" where a man's body was stretched up. His arms went up into each section of the "X" and there he was crucified.
- There was another cross. It was a straight tree, with a spike. They pushed the man's body on it and turned it any old way they liked—like a propeller—and left him to hang and the birds to eat him.

There's another crucifixion worse than any of them. That was, that if you murdered someone, they would take that dead body of the person you murdered and they would crucify you to the body—to the dead body! There's a thought! They made you lay down on it. They strapped your arms to the other arms; your legs to the other legs; your trunk to the other trunk; your neck to that neck. Then they stood you up and said, "Get going!" You staggered everywhere with a body of death!

Gradually, of course, it became rigid with death. The mortification! The stench! The flesh, the whole body would degenerate! You would try to sleep with that rotten thing. If you were stumbling down the road after two or three days, the stench had made you vomit and you were just about as sick and weak and feeling as horrid as you could. You saw a friend and cried, "Hey Jack! Cut this body off from me!" Whispering, "OK. There's nobody around." He gets his knife out and cuts the ropes off. He's just going to cut the last one. You look up and there's a Roman sentry: "What are you doing?" "I'm liberating my friend." "The law doesn't allow you to do that." "Oh, yes it does, yes it does, yes it does." "Go ahead, on one condition. The one condition is that if you free that man from that corpse, that corpse will be tied to your body. Do you love him enough now to have the body...?" "Oh no, sir! I won't cut it. I don't want that stinking rotten corpse attached to my body!" "All right. We'll tie him up again..."

Now Paul had been talking about the Law in chapter 7.

- He says the Law is holy.
- He says the Law is spiritual.

But, you see, the Law could bring condemnation. It could point out sin, but it couldn't cast out sin. Can the Law break you free? No. Who shall deliver me from this wretched man? *"Who shall deliver me from the body of this death?"* He says there's no end to this! But then he says, "Yes there is... Thanks be unto God through Jesus Christ my Lord...!" Romans 6:6 says that *"Knowing this, that our old man* ***is*** *(not was, but* ***is****) crucified with Him."*

- The trouble in the church of God today is that we preach half a salvation.
- We tell people how to get rid of the lousy sin, yet we don't tell them
- how to get rid of the principle inside that has dominion over them.
- This is exactly what Paul is talking about in this epistle.
- This is why I say it's the song of the soul set free.

Come over to verse 9. *"You are not in the flesh, but in the Spirit."* Are you in the Spirit? Or in the flesh? Have you got secrets? What's biting you on the inside? **An unforgiving spirit? A grudge? Laziness? Jealousy? Anger? Secret lusts? What is it?**

He says,

Ye are not in the flesh, but in the Spirit, if so be..."

Now listen!

"...the Spirit of God dwelleth in you!"

Look at the next verse (verse 10):

"If Christ be in you."

Look at the 11th verse:

"The spirit of Him that raised up Jesus...dwell in you."

My! Oh my! How can you be indwelt by

God the Father,

God the Son, and

God the Holy Ghost

and be defeated?!

Don't argue with me about it. Scratch it out in your Bible if you don't believe it. If you're a Christian, you're an indwelt person.

- God dwells in you.
- The Father dwells in you.

That's what it says. I didn't write that. The Holy Ghost wrote it. I want you to know: if you're really born of God, God dwells in you. And the Son dwells in you. "*He that hath the Son hath life; he that hath not the Son...*" It doesn't matter if they baptized you three times a day, it won't make you a Christian. Who is a Christian?

He that hath the Son.

He that is born of God, and

He that hath the Spirit of God dwelling in him.

All right. Let's come down a bit further in the chapter. Look at verse 22. "*We know that the whole creation groaneth and travaileth in pain together...*" Do you think it is doing that tonight? Men have dreamed of Utopia. And I'm going to tell you how many more. Hitler said you could dominate the world by a pure race. The Marxists say the only way to clean the world up is to get rid of the fluff and bourgeois folk we have around here and rule by revolution. The creation groaneth.

The whole creation groaneth! Did it cost you a tear when you heard that fifty million people were signed off in Vietnam, Laos, and Cambodia? Fifty million people went into captivity! Did it cost you a tear? Millions of people behind the Iron Curtain. Has it cost you a tear? -- or are you still rehearsing your choir number for Sunday? Yes, I believe every earthquake we have, is a sign of the whole groaning creation. **Creation groans.**

Will you notice what Paul says a little further down? In the next verse, verse 23: **that we, not only creation, but <u>we ourselves</u> also have the first fruits of the Spirit. If you have the first fruits of the Spirit, here's the proof that you have it. That you groan within yourself.** Do you? After the Holy Ghost comes in—and He knows the mind of God, and nobody does but the Spirit—the Spirit whispers the secret of God to you. Some nights you're like the woman who wants to get delivered of something. It isn't time, and you groan within yourself.

You can't learn groaning except by the Holy Ghost. It's the school of the Holy Spirit.

If you think that's unusual, then look at verse 26 in which he says, *"Likewise the Spirit helpeth our infirmities, for we know not what we should pray for as we ought, but the Spirit itself maketh intercession for us with GROANINGS that cannot be uttered."* And verse 27, *"the Spirit... because maketh intercession...according to the will of God."*

Now, I've heard people say that to pray "with groanings," means praying in tongues. It's nothing of the kind. Because if it was, God would say so. It's beyond that.

The greatest language of prayer has no vocabulary.

The greatest prayers in the Bible have no words.

Do you remember Hannah? How she prayed? Even the man of God, the priest, thought she was drunk. She groaned. She travailed. She was barren.

When the Holy Ghost comes and begins to burden people, it's a pretty, pretty rough thing to learn the true language of intercession. But the Spirit helpeth our infirmity.

Let's come to this verse right here for a minute or two. *"In all these things..."* He mentions them. Sort them out when you go home, will you? **Tribulation, distress, famine, peril, nakedness, sword, perils of the deep, and so forth and so on. Sort them out. You'll find that**

Some are things that attack the body.
Some attack the mind.
Some attack the spirit.

And he says, *"In all these things..."* There is no area in your life where, as a Christian, you are expected to be defeated.

You say, "I can't be perfect." Can't you? Are you sure? Jesus said in the Sermon on the Mount, *"Be ye therefore perfect."* He said of Job to the devil, *"Hast thou considered my servant Job? He's perfect and upright."* He set a path for Abraham before the Holy Ghost was given as we know. He said, *"Walk before me and be thou perfect."* You can't have

Adamic perfection in your body. You can't have mental perfection. You can't have perfection, but you CAN have perfect obedience.

We sing the song, *"Perfect submission. All is at rest."* The only way you can have rest is by perfect submission—to know there's no rebellion in your spirit in any area at all.

"In all these things we are more than conquerors." You know, very often we get so discouraged. We get so earthbound. We lose sight of the majesty of God. We forget this: that God has branded you as a child of God. He lives in you. His Spirit lives in you. Christ lives in you. And we let little rubbish around us upset us?

Then he says in Romans 9:33, *"Who shall lay anything to the charge of God's elect? It is God that justifieth."* Here is your strength. Notice in this verse again, verse 34: *"Who is he that condemneth? It is Christ that died."* Can Christ's death be contested? Satan knows better than that. Then says, he *"is risen again...at the right hand..."* Can the sovereignty of Jesus Christ be contested? And at the end of the verse it says, he "maketh intercession for us." Is there any way that the prayers of Jesus Christ can be sabotaged?

In Washington - in the Smithsonian museum, I guess, there's a bit of an apron with a dirty brown mark on it. And the Rockefellers have a bit of money and yet the Rockefellers can't buy that apron. It looks like a chocolate stain and the apron isn't worth much. But when they were carrying the great emancipator Lincoln out of that theater, as they passed a little girl, his blood fell on that apron and immediately somebody said, "that is sacred for America, get hold of it." There's nothing in the world can buy that thing which is stamped with blood! And I want to tell you tonight in the face of the world, the flesh, and the devil and all hell that if the blood of Jesus Christ is on you tonight you're worth more than all the wealth in Fort Knox or anywhere else in the world. You're precious to Him... Why?... Because His blood is upon you, that's why.

What are you going to do with this text? What is this text? "In all these things," verse 37, "we are more than conquerors." That's beyond the bounds of logic. How can you be **MORE** than a conqueror?

You can do three things with this text. You can say,

"It's a statement by an ignorant, irresponsible person. The kind who overload you with confidence."

You can say, "It's an unbalanced statement by a super-optimist."

Or you can say is, "Here's a man talking out of experience."

"In all these things," he says, "we are more than conquerors."

You see, the Holy Spirit is so wonderful:

- He's a spirit of truth and He convicts us of error.
- He's a spirit of life and He convicts of death.
- He's a spirit of power and He convicts of weakness.
- He's a spirit of joy and He convicts of sorrow.
- And He's a spirit of <u>love</u>!

You see, we've got the idea that you've got to be anointed of the Holy Ghost to be a missionary or a preacher. Well, that's great. You must have that. Let me tell you about three things here. Look. This man says we are more than conquerors. You know, when those three Hebrew children went into a burning, fiery furnace, they were conquerors. But when the form of the fourth, like unto the Son of God, came and they walked out, they were MORE THAN CONQUERORS.

When Daniel went into the lion's den, he was a conqueror.

But when they pulled him out and made them change the laws of the Medes and the Persians, he was <u>more than a conqueror.</u>

When Jesus went to the cross, He could have just went "Pffft!" like that, and destroyed every man that was living. He could have cursed these people like He cursed the fig tree. But He kept His mouth shut. When He went to the grave with the sin of the world He was a conqueror.

<u>When He rose from the dead he was more than a conqueror</u>. That's why this marvelous 8th chapter is so majestic. The Spirit of Him that raised up Jesus from the dead." Has he raised you from the dead? And touched death? And trespasses? And sin? Has He raised you from the death of formality and self-righteousness? If He has, you're indwelt by God the Father! You're indwelt by God the Son! You're indwelt by the Holy Ghost!

You know what America needs more than it needs some revivalist? It needs some Holy-Ghost filled mothers and Holy-Ghost filled fathers. I owe my spiritual life after God to a saintly SS Teacher who influenced my life. I never heard her gossip. I never heard her criticize anybody. I never saw her get angry. I can hear her singing, "Take Time to Be Holy," usually off-key. But she was singing "Take Time to Be Holy." If it wasn't that, it was "Trust and Obey."

Outside of the New Testament, the greatest thing I ever read was the life of David Brainerd. I read that when he was about 18 years of age, he met God. I read that he died at the age of 28. The ripe old age of 28! I read that he used to kneel in the snow when it was up to his chin, when he had to make a hole in it. And, pray! He said, "I'd pray from sunrise to sunset. I couldn't touch the snow with the tips of my fingers. The heat of my body melted the snow." He had tuberculosis and when he sneezed he sprayed the snow with his blood.

Friend, listen. **You have only one life.**

T'will will soon be passed.

Only what's done for God will last.

So now,

1. Die to self-seeking.
2. Die to public opinion.
3. Die to ambition.
    - **God doesn't use men that are alive. He uses men that are dead.**
    - **He doesn't use sober men. He uses drunk men.**
    - **He doesn't use somebody. He uses nobody.**

"In all these things..." Where's your point of defeat? - Is it prayerlessness? - Is it lack of love? - Is it self-pity? - Self-seeking? - Self-glory? - Self-promoting? What is it? -- You may be the one key holding up revival. Maybe just you, nobody else. I don't know. -- I want to tell you, God can put an end to all these things and you can leave this house tonight free, if you obey God. You can be more than conquerors by the indwelling God, by the indwelling Holy Spirit of God. But you'll have to confess it. I can't confess it for you. If I could repent for you, I'd be down there right now repenting for you. I can't do it. You have to do it. God can't do it for you. <u>You</u> have to do it.

BREAKING THROUGH TO THE HEAVENLIES

Matthew 6:6-13

But thou, when thou prayest, enter into thy closet, and when thou hast shut thy door, pray to thy Father which is in secret; and thy Father which seeth in secret shall reward thee openly. [7] But when ye pray, use not vain repetitions, as the heathen do: for they think that they shall be heard for their much speaking. [8] Be not ye therefore like unto them: for your Father knoweth what things ye have need of, before ye ask him. [9] After this manner therefore pray ye:

Our Father which art in heaven, Hallowed be thy name. [10] Thy kingdom come. Thy will be done in earth, as it is in heaven. [11] Give us this day our daily bread. [12] And forgive us our debts, as we forgive our debtors. [13] And lead us not into temptation, but deliver us from evil: For thine is the kingdom, and the power, and the glory, forever. Amen.

Matthew 6:6-13

"But thou, when thou prayest,..."

1. *I cannot say our if religion has no room for others and their needs.*
2. *I cannot say Father if I do not demonstrate this relationship in my daily living.*
3. *I cannot say who art in heaven if all my interests and pursuits are on earthly things.*

4. *I cannot say hallowed be thy name if I, who am called by his name, am not holy.*
5. *I cannot* say thy kingdom come *if I am unwilling to give up my own sovereignty and accept the righteous reign of God.*
6. *I cannot say thy will be done if I am unwilling or resentful of having it in my life.*
7. *I cannot say in earth as it is in heaven unless I am truly ready to give myself to his service here and now.*
8. *I cannot say give us this day our daily bread without expending honest effort for it or by ignoring the genuine needs of my fellowmen.*
9. *I cannot say forgive us our trespasses as we forgive those who trespass against us if I continue to harbor a grudge against anyone.*
10. *I cannot say lead us not into temptation if I deliberately choose to remain in a situation where I am likely to be tempted.*
11. *I cannot say deliver us from evil if I am not prepared to fight in the spiritual realm with the weapon of prayer.*
12. *I cannot say thine is the kingdom if I do not give the King the disciplined obedience of a loyal subject.*
13. *I cannot say thine is the power if I fear what my neighbors may say or do.*
14. *I cannot say thine is the glory if I am seeking my own glory first.*

It's hard to talk about prayer -- there is a tendency to absorb so much with our minds that It hinders our spirits grasping the reality that is beyond the surface.

It's so easy to have the letter about the Spirit and forget that the letter, even if it's about the Spirit, is not the Spirit.

The inner essence is beyond the letter, beyond the feelings, beyond the mind, beyond
the intellect. The Spiritual essence gives life.

In our scripture Jesus, responding to His disciple's request, is giving them a way to pray, and He says "after this manner."

It's not the words, it's something beyond the words

- It's the whole concept,
- It's the spirit,
- It's the attitude,
- It's the steps of prayer that are laid down here.

The Lord has been taking me back to some things that I thought I knew well and showing me that they were not exactly what I thought they were. Prayer is one of those things. The Lord's prayer is one of those prayers.

"Our Father." It's the beginning of the relationship. I do not think we can overemphasize this. He has to be our Father. God never deals with us in a cold relationship. There has to be something more than that.

There has to be something living; there has to be something warm -- a love relationship, a knowledge of who He is.

The One with whom I have relationship,

- The One who is faithful, with the immensity of heaven's fullness,
- The One who is faithful and true to His purpose in my life.

As He leads me through places that my mind can't understand. As He leads me through places where my feelings cannot follow - and if He is going to lead me He is going to lead me through all those places - then this must undergird.

There are two things we need to know about God:

- One, that He loves us,
- Two, that He understands us.

He is faithful, He is true - **He is our Father**.

The brilliant scientist Sir Isaac Newton said that he could take his telescope and look millions and millions of miles into space. Then he added, *"But when I lay it aside, go into my room, shut the door, and get down on my knees in earnest prayer, I see more of Heaven and feel closer to the Lord than if I were assisted by all the telescopes on earth."*

Some people go all through life understanding in their mind, and it never ever filters down to their heart.

- Never becomes something that upholds,
- Never transmits light from within upon the rest of our circumstances, upon the rest of our limitations, upon the rest of our battles.

We must see past the natural.
A missionary with lots of years of experience, told me, *"Alton, you need to see beyond the second causes. You need to see the spiritual. There is nothing apart from the spiritual. Everything is spiritual."*

Beyond a hard meeting, beyond a rebellious child, beyond a difficult work situation, beyond all the earthly things, we need to see the spiritual.

Beyond even the need, and the lack, and the want, and the supply, and all those things, we need to see the spiritual.

Beyond all things there is a spiritual reason.
"The kingdoms of this world," it says at the end of the Bible, "are become the kingdoms of our God and of His Christ." Until they do the Kingdom of God and the kingdom of the enemy are warring and there is no other real seat of power. It is either God or the enemy.

The great tragedy of life is not unanswered prayer, but unoffered prayer. -- F.B. Meyer

---

"Our Father which art in Heaven."

I used to read this and think, *"Well, He is a Heavenly Father, He is up above, He's got a realm of power which is above earth."* But I think there is something more than that. As the years go by, I am seeing that God, through many circumstances, through tremendous pressures, teaches the soul the enormous distance that there is between earth and heaven. The enormous distance that I must travel if I am going to get to heaven.

Somebody explained once in a meeting, *"Well, God's in heaven, man's on earth. God has conquered on the cross, everything is all right. Just bring your request to God. He knows what you need before you ask, so just say, 'Lord I need this and I need that, and it's done.'"* Well, it's not done... there must be a balance in this whole thing. There is a lot of teaching that would present God as man's helper. The teaching seems to imply, God is here to help you. God is here to lead you. God is here to make sure that your life is a success - *"Realizing your potential," "You are loved"*...that whole idea. There is a part of that, but as far as I'm concerned, it's very much on the periphery. Just compare it with the magnitude which God wants us to get in the spiritual.

Jim Elliot, a missionary slain by the Auca Indians in the 1950's, once said: God is still on His throne and man is still on his footstool. There's only a knee's distance in between.

I am just starting to realize a little bit of <u>where</u> God calls me to, <u>how far</u> it is, and <u>how hard</u> it is to get there.

The missionary that I mentioned had a wonderful ministry. People used to say, "Oh, he has such a grace. It seems that he just comes and gives God's bounty to us, just flows and the people weep and cry and they are overwhelmed. It's glorious!" But one thing they did not realize was **where he had to go** to get that. **How far** he had to go. With all his years of experience, he would spend hours seeking God before an hour meeting! He would come to the meeting having made a long, long, journey. I think many times our problem is that we quit.

THE CHILD ON EARTH HAS GOT TO GO TO HEAVEN
IF HE IS GOING TO GET HIS PRAYERS ANSWERED.

I think it was one of the old Puritans, who said words to this effect, "God will not refuse the answer to any man's prayer who goes to heaven with his need."

- I've got to get beyond a self-seeking and a self-interest.
- I've got to get beyond an earthly concept of the thing.

If it's a selfish prayer I'll never get to heaven with it.

- *Once I leave the earth, the selfishness which is of the earth stays in the earth.*

You follow what I mean? The hang-ups, the complexes, the doubts, the fears, all of those things are of earth. I reach through to heaven. It means I go beyond all earthly things and I get into that place where their influence cannot reach. **I get into His presence**. This is the challenge that God puts before us.

- We are called to pray in the Spirit.
- We are called to reach through to the heavenlies.

That is the place where we possess our inheritance.

"Hallowed by Thy name."

The Spanish Bible says, ***"Your name be sanctified."*** I believe it's practically the same. **It means separated.** We tend to bring God down and mix Him in with our earthly scene. It says, "Be your name separated."

- God's Kingdom and man's kingdom do not mix.
- God and the devil do not mix,
- God's nature and man's nature do not mix either.

"Hallowed be Thy name." Be Thy name separated in my thinking. That God's name be set on a high and holy pinnacle unreachable for all else. Separate from every other thing:

- All my religious drives, all my religious ambitions.
- All my desires that God would bless me, that God would work through me.
- All those things must be set to one side.

Let there be no taint in my life on the name of God. Remember one of the first commandments, ***"Thou shalt not take the name of the Lord thy God in vain."*** It's not just swearing or anything of the sort; it's not just sinning in the sense of outward sins.

It's taking something of God and not realizing the potential of that which we have taken. It's like having a 200 horsepower car and never exceeding 15 miles an hour. It's in vain to have a motor that can reach 100 miles an hour and never go more than 15 miles an hour. Likewise, it's in vain to take all of heaven and apply it to my poor miserable life, so that I feel free, so that I feel happy, so I don't have hang-ups, and I'm not condemned dragging a sense of guilt.

You know, we are so limited. We are like the horses with the blinders on. We look in one direction. We see one thing. We follow a path that others have marked out for us. God wants to set us free.

We are like painters that paint miniatures -- tiny little paintings. Maybe in that little painting they have a whole landscape. They paint hills, mountains, a lake, a village over on the far side, people skating on the lake, birds overhead, rushes, flowers, everything in that tiny little painting.

I think that is what we do with God, we try to reduce it all down. "Oh, here is God, all the fullness of God, look, there are mountains, there are lakes, there... you know."

Here's another gem from Howard Hendricks: *For Sunday School Teachers,*

"Years ago in a church in Dallas we were having trouble finding a teacher for a junior high boys class. The list of prospects had only one name -- and when they told me who it was I said, "You've got to be kidding." But I couldn't have been more wrong about that young man. He took the class and revolutionized it.

I was so impressed I invited him to my home for lunch and asked him the secret of his success. He pulled out a little black book. On each page he had a small picture of one of the boys, and under the boy's name were comments like "having trouble in arithmetic," or "comes to church against parents' wishes," or "would like to be a missionary someday, but doesn't think he has what it takes."

"I pray over those pages every day," he said, "and I can hardly wait to come to church each Sunday to see what God has been doing in their lives."

Or say it another way, we live in a Lilliputian world. You've read the book of Gulliver and Lilliput, the man that went and lived among tiny little people. I think the average Christian is something like that. Tiny little things that are our enemies -- we get so fearful.

A tiny little enemy and the child of God is going to pieces. On the other hand he has a tiny little victory over a tiny little thing and, "Oh, I feel so good."

You've seen these people that hear a new teaching or some little thing and they have a tiny dimension of truth, and you ask, "How are you?" "Oh, brother! Yesterday I learned Jesus loves me." Well, that's great, but we ought to know that and we ought to be going on.

God does not paint miniatures. The **dimension of God is universal**. I think we are going to find out many things when we get to heaven, but one of the things is that eternity is not only a line that goes on without end. That it's not only year after year and century after century; it's not a line of time. I think we are going to find out that eternity is as broad as it is long. There is a dimension of fullness there that we can't begin to understand. Paul says to one of the churches that they might understand the length and breadth and depth and height. In **everything** God does He wants to lead us through to a greater realm of the spirit and give us something beyond.

"Hallowed be Thy name." Thy name be set apart and not reduced to my world of miniatures. We need to pray that. We need to pray, *"God be Your name hallowed* *in my life,* *set apart from every earthly influence, and power, and concept and feeling. Be Your name put up there so that I start to find a God who is above it all, a God who is over it all. A God who is finally the Lord of Lords and King of Kings. It starts with His faithfulness, it starts out with His reality within, but it goes on and on with His fullness and omnipotence. God over and above and beyond it all.*

"Thy Kingdom come."

Over against the kingdom of the enemy, "Thy Kingdom come." After we'd been in different areas of the country, different meetings, seen a measure of God's blessing, God's moving, God's anointing, we went over to another place. A bunch of people had come over to help. The same kind of meetings, the same people in a different place. We'd sing the same songs. We'd preach and we'd pray with the same intensity, the same faith. Yet every prayer, every song, would seem to hit the wall and bounce down on to the floor. I remember once in a meeting we were singing and it just came to me -- it wasn't a vision, it wasn't a voice, but just as clear as if it had been -- that

- Every sickness, every sin,
- Every sorrow, every wrong,
- Every hurt, every pain,

All the suffering of that place multiplied by the thousands and millions of people,

1. Multiplied by its generations,
2. Multiplied by each individual decision in wrong
3. And each temptation,

Every single crooked thing, every hurt against God had somehow, in the invisible world, taken on substance and become material. And in the spiritual world, as though those things had turned into bricks, the enemy had built a fortress.

Have you seen any of those castles in Europe? Walls that go on and on, tremendously high, tremendously broad, towers, turrets, courtyards, moats, that whole tremendous dimension of an impregnable fortress. Well, it's somewhat like that. It seemed in that meeting as though in my mind's eye I could see the devil up on top of this tremendous fortress. And he was saying, "As surely as I exist you shall not enter in." As the Bible says about Israel, we were like a little flock of goats in front of the forces of the enemy. A tiny insignificant group of people. Yet, at the same time, there was a sense of another Voice coming and saying, *"In My name you shall go against this and you shall go in."* Two realities.

And so the prayer is: "**Thy** Kingdom come." Because the other kingdom does exist. The other kingdom is real and is powerful. It's not an abstract kingdom.

It doesn't matter whether I believe it or I don't believe it. It exists, it's real. God wants to get us to see this. We know it mentally yet many times we act as though it weren't true. Many times you see Christians that are like a yo-yo. They seem to be at the end of a string of feeling that go up and down, up and down -- Now they are condemned, now they aren't, now they are. Only a contact with God, with the eternal dimension of God, will get us free from this.
"Thy Kingdom come."... it starts with us - it starts with this commitment:

"Thy will be done."

His will, not ours, be done on earth. The apostle says, "He who labors must be the first partaker of the fruits." As I pray, *"Thy will be done on earth,"*

<u>It starts with this earth that I am</u> - the earth I am made out of.

It's a prayer that I pray first of all for myself,

1. "God, Your will be done on this earth which I am."
2. "God, in Your way.
3. God, in Your time.
4. God, at whatever price You ordain."

God is always out beyond the end of what I know, or what I can bear, or what I think my consecration involves. One thing is to talk about and trust God. Another thing is when you have to face the darkness and see that the nature of darkness is not as you had in mind,

- It works in a different way,
- It comes in from behind,
- It invades different areas,

Then I have to insist on this:

"Thy will be done on earth as it is in heaven."
This is the dimension. Not just Thy will be done on earth. God doesn't let us off that easy. "Thy will be done on earth ***as it is in heaven***." Do you realize what He's saying?

If I were an angel in heaven and God wanted to do something through me, to what extent would He do it? Could I go back to God and say, "Lord, I would have liked to have done it more fully but circumstances would not permit?"
His will as in heaven -

a. There is no coloration through human personality.
b. There is no limitation through the pressure of circumstances,
c. There is no frustration; there is no delay.

This is the measure that God wants us to reach, not only in our seeing but in our believing. "Lord, Your will be done in this earth as it is in heaven."

a. "Well, when I get to heaven, I'm going to praise the Lord."
b. "I am going to sing; it won't matter who sees me; nothing will matter."
c. "I am going to give Him perfect praise when I get to heaven."

Then the Lord comes and says, "Child, why not now?" Well, is there anything hindering? Is there?

"No, nothing... apart from my feelings...

- And My Human Personality...
- And The Folks Around Me...
- And That I Don't Want To Make A Fool Of Myself..." Right?

God says,

> "You can present on earth your prayers, your praises, your worship, your service, in the same essential reality that you are going to present them in heaven."

I'm sure we'll have glorified voices, all the rusty overtones will be taken away, great! But will the heart be any different? Will death suddenly transform us and endue us with all perfection? I think there is a growth all through eternity, but the desire, the giving, can be just as much ours here as there. Lord, I want to follow you all the way. Can I do any more than that even in heaven? I can't.

God wants us to be wise enough to understand that through faith we take limited abilities and we make them unlimited. Because faith takes hold of God.

Just as we go to heaven with our prayers,
Taking the earthly into the heavenly,
So in all our life

- There must be that contact,
- There must be that reality,
- There must be that flow

… otherwise all is death, death, death. It can be a cold death, or it can be wild, shouting, singing, stomping death. It's all the same. The only thing that God is interested in is reality.

Nothing more glorious than to get to the end of life, or get to the end of a day, or even to the end of a meeting and say, "God, I've done what you wanted me to do. Lord, I believed I opened my being that You might flow through me."

There is something within us all that is withdrawn and unbelieving

- Unbelief is not just the absence of belief.
- Unbelief is the presence of something destructive.

The Bible talks about an evil heart of unbelief. It talks about not having obtained the grace - *"Beware… lest any man fail of the grace of God, lest a root of bitterness springing up…"* Beware, if there is not <u>this,</u> then there will be <u>that</u>. If you don't reach the grace you will reach the bitterness.

This grace is the dimension of victory.
This is the release of our personality.
This is coming into God.

We don't realize our purpose or find the realization of our life by seeking after it. That is incidental. We find it in God, in our Father which is in heaven.
We find it in learning to pray this prayer again. Hallowing His name, pleading for His Kingdom to come.

"Give us this day our daily bread."

It refers to that which we eat for our physical wellbeing, but it's far beyond that. It's what we eat for our spiritual wellbeing – Spiritual bread. Give us this day our spiritual portion.

"Give us this day our daily bread." ***There must be this expectation.*** "God, You have promised and I am going to wait with a waiting that is filled with faith."

A faith which although it doesn't have a voice is saying, "God, God, God." Right through the day.

As though my heart was there in His presence saying, "Lord I want it, I want it, I need it, I need it..." It's a maintaining. Not an audible voice, but an inner cry before God. "Give us **this** day."

"Lord, do not let this day finish without me finding on earth what you have released in heaven for me. Lord, let the communication be open again."

"Forgive us our debt as we forgive our debtors."

There are certain things which are conditional. A verse that has been very important through the years is II Corinthians 10:6. It says, *"When your obedience is fulfilled, God will avenge all disobedience."* Before that it talks about the weapons of our warfare being "not carnal, but mighty through God for the pulling down of strong holds." The weapons are mighty... but the strongholds are pulled down when our obedience is fulfilled.

1. You cannot say the Lord's prayer,
   and even once say "I".
2. You cannot pray the Lord's prayer,
   and even once say "My".
3. Nor can you pray the Lord's prayer
   and not pray for another.
4. For when you ask for daily bread,
   you must include your brother!
5. For others are included in each and every plea.
6. From the beginning to the end of it.
   it does not once say "me".

I remember many years ago now, the Lord talking to me about certain areas of my life: "When it's all in order, then I will do."

God will finish all that I cannot do. In other words, I can reach so far and I have to reach that far. My obedience must be fulfilled, but when I reach as far as I can reach then He will take it from there.

1. He'll never leave us -- His presence will be there.
2. He'll never forsake us -- His abundance and provision will always be there.

"Forgive us our debts as we forgive our debtors."

It's a big thing to have the heart changed to such an extent that the only thing that flows from me to other people is positive.

- That I do not have hurt that I close up inside.
- That I don't have a debt with people in my feelings or in any other realm.
- That toward them I give as God gives.

"And lead us not into temptation... deliver us from evil."

Somebody said, "There are two parts to this: Keep me from the moment of temptation, because I am going to fall, but farther *TRANSFORM* me so that evil will not touch me." Remember Jesus just before He died said, "The enemy will come, but will find nothing in Me." It is a great thing to get to a place where the enemy can't tempt me. You know, I'm not tempted to take something I don't like.

Our trouble is that so many times we give a mental assent to certain things. With that we think that they are done and they are not. I think many times of the mystics, some of the old saints who for years and years sought God, went through anguish and suffering to come into faith. Our tendency in the twentieth century is to read about those lives and think,

"Oh, poor so and so, he sought for years and years to come into a real peace with God. He could not just trust in God, and believe in the love of God."

Think of Martin Luther fighting there until he finally came to believe that he was justified by faith. Or John Wesley striving and disciplining himself and doing every conceivable thing until at last he reached through to salvation. **BUT** when they did reach through, Wesley changed a nation, and Luther changed the course of history. If it takes 15 years, better 15 years of darkness preparing me to see the Light than a 15 minute experience which can't even keep my nose above water when the enemy comes to condemn me or to tempt me or to confuse me.

1. We cannot see the Light until we have seen the darkness,
2. We cannot see the positive until we have seen the negative,
3. We cannot see the fullness of God until we have seen our need of that fullness.

We cannot -- it's impossible. We need some frame of reference.

Have you ever seen a photo, maybe a beautiful picture of a water fall? You looked at it and said, "Well, how big is that waterfall?" There are some ferns up close... "Is it no bigger than those ferns? Is it a lot bigger?" There is no reference. Sometimes in technical books they will put a ruler there beside the photo. We need a perspective.

One of the mystics, Pascal, used to talk about the disproportion of mankind. The disproportion in man's thinking. The disproportion of everything human. We got it out of proportion. Only God can put it back into proportion. Only God can show us where it's at.

It ends up saying,

1. **"For Thine is the Kingdom."** - The authority, the rule.
2. **"Thine is the Power."** - The ability to transmit that authority and that rule.
3. **"Thine is the Glory."** - Not just for time, but forever.

We are privileged to form a part of eternity, even on earth. I am sure that every single thing that God gives us, every gift, every word, every promise, every deliverance, every little bit of light on the Scripture, every sign along life's road, is part of eternity.

As the enemy built up spiritual oppression through the hurt and through the wrong, so God in our lives, day after day, week after week, month after month, year after year, wants to build up.

- Let's not let go of what God gives us.
- Let's seek to participate of the Kingdom and of the Power and of the Glory of God.

I remember many, many years ago, one of the first times I'd seen the Spirit of God sweep into a place. They started singing, "It's a glorious church without spot or wrinkle," maybe some of the older people know it. They sang and it was just as if the words were clothed with meaning. Clothed with a feeling and clothed with a security and a partaking of something eternal. "It's a glorious church." Why? Because God had come.

There is not very much glory around, is there? Certainly God wants to lead us on into this. There is a whole pathway of prayer. A whole pathway of life. We learn to pray it until we can pray it in reality. If we reach the end of our lives and we are able at the end to pray this prayer with meaning, believe me, we will have gone a long, long way in God. When it all means something here in the heart, we'll have gone a long, long way in God.

- There will have been many earthly things left behind.
- There will be many battles gained; many things that won't even be able to touch us anymore.
- There will be much awareness, and much closeness, much revelation, and much light, and much glory from the heavenly Kingdom flooding our souls.

When God brings you into tremendous situations suddenly you realize they can only go so far, they cannot reach beyond, they cannot touch me, I'm behind that line. Things may come and fill my whole horizon, but within they can't touch a single thing. The Kingdom of God within is untouchable. What is it Peter says? That we have an inheritance that fadeth not away, undefiled, reserved in heaven for us.

God leads on from faith to faith, but He leads us on in many other realms too. He leads us on from light to light... glory to glory... victory to victory... life to life, on and on for ever. All His world is just an exploding world. Have you seen pictures of a little bud when it's filmed and speeded up and it just bursts into flower? That's how our life is in God. God wants everything to open up more and more. For Thine is the Kingdom... it doesn't belong to the devil, doesn't belong to mankind.

If I reach through, and I've finally been able to shrug it all off,

> The good and the bad,
> That which is mine which belongs to this earth,
> That which belongs to the devil,

<u>Then</u> I come to this: **"For Thine is the Kingdom."** Not up there only, but here.
<u>"Lord, do all that's lacking -- I have done my part and</u>

Thine is the Kingdom, Thine is the power, Thine is the glory forever.
Amen."

If all the sleeping folk will wake up,
If all the lukewarm folk will fire up,
If all the dishonest folk will confess up,
If all the disgruntled folk will cheer up,
If all the depressed folk will cheer up,
If all the estranged folk will make up,
If all the gossipers will shut up,
If all true soldiers will stand up,
If all the dry bones will shake up,
If all the church members will pray up...
Then we can have a revival! – R.G. Lee

Resurrection of Jesus

God's Wonderful Game Plan

What would you do if you were a high school football player whose coach sent in a play, which called for you to run the ball to your opponent's end zone and score for the other team? It has happened!

With 7 seconds left in the game, Tishomingo High School was leading Falkner High School, 16-14. At stake was a birth in Mississippi's 1988-state class 1A playoffs. Tishomingo had the ball on Falkner's 40-yard line. All they had to do was run out the clock on the next play, and they would win the game by two points.

Coach David Herbert, who has Lou Gehrig's disease and coaches from a seat in the back of a pickup truck, sent in a play to his son and the team's quarterback, Dave Herbert. The play called for a handoff to tailback Shane Hill and for him to run as fast as he could for the other team's end zone and score.

"Your daddy must be crazy!" protested one of the tackles. So, while the argument went on in the team's huddle, a delay-of-game penalty was called on Tishomingo. Finally, the team lined up, the ball was handed off to the tailback, and he ran 55 yards in the "wrong" direction. He laid down in the opponent's end zone and waited for the clock to expire with practically everyone on the field and in the stadium bewildered. The results were a two-point safety for Falkner. Score tied. Time expired.

Was the coach crazy? Was he out of his mind for calling such a play? You see, in order for his team to reach the playoffs, Tishomingo had to beat Falkner by 4 or more points. After thinking about the chances of going 40 yards on one play or kicking a field goal from that distance, he decided overtime was his best bet.

What was the result of the coach's play? Tishomingo won in overtime, 22-16, on a third down, two-yard run by Shane Hill. Hill finished the game with minus 29 yards for the night. But his team won and went to the playoffs.

1. This story sounds a bit like the cross to me. God became a man, was pushed around by His enemies, and was executed as a criminal by the Roman governor of Palestine. Satan appeared to have won. Jesus of Nazareth was dead. His disciples were scattered. On the surface, it seemed that God had suffered defeat. Or had He?

2. Three days later, Jesus was alive from the dead. Over a period of 40 days, He showed Himself alive to hundreds of people. Then, 51 days later, Peter explained that it had all been part of a divine strategy.

He said, in (Acts 2:23) "This man was handed over to you by God's set purpose and foreknowledge; and you, with the help of wicked men, put Him to death by nailing Him to the cross."

3. He continued and cited Old Testament predictions, which had been fulfilled by the resurrection.

4. The finale came when he announced, "God has make this Jesus, whom you crucified, both Lord and Christ" (Acts 2:36).

5. There you have it! A game plan that looked to the entire world like craziness. One, which still mystifies disciples in our church-huddles and observers in the world-stadium alike. But the Son executed His father's call to perfection. He died on the cross to take care of our sin problem and was raised from the dead. Through God's perfect plan, through God's perfect strategy, which looked foolish to the onlookers, we have become victorious--we have become winners.

6. Unfortunately, though, there are many people today who still will not believe in the cross and in the resurrection of Jesus. They think it is absurd to believe in something that far feted. They try to explain that the resurrection never occurred and that we are all fools for believing it.

7. Well, ladies and gentleman, call me a fool. Because I believe with all my heart in the resurrection of Jesus Christ.

"For the message of the cross is foolishness to those who are perishing, but to us who are being saved it is the power of God" (1 Cor. 1:18)."

WE ARE GOING TO EXAMINE GOD'S GAME PLAN BY LOOKING AT THE RESURRECTION OF JESUS CHRIST.

I. FIRST, WITHOUT A DOUBT, JESUS WAS RESURRECTED FROM THE DEAD.

1. As I told you earlier, many people do not believe in Jesus' resurrection.

2. Here are several arguments people use to support their position.

A. SOME CRITICS ARGUE THAT THE RESURRECTION WAS A HOAX BY SUGGESTING THAT JESUS DID NOT ACTUALLY DIE ON THE CROSS.

1. This theory (which is known as the swoon theory) teaches that Jesus only appeared dead but was revived later in the tomb.

2. I do not buy this theory, and I'll tell you why...

a. Before Jesus was placed on the cross...

(1) The Bible tells us in (Mt. 27:26) that He was flogged which means He was whipped 39 times with leather throngs that contained jagged pieces of bone and lead.

(2) Dr. C. Truman Davis, a medical doctor who has meticulously studied crucifixion from a medical perspective, describes the effects of a flogging. "The heavy whip is brought down with full force again and again

across (a person's) shoulders, back and legs. At first the heavy thongs cut through the skin only. Then, as the blows continue, they cut deeper into the tissues, producing first an oozing of blood from the veins of the skin, and finally spurting arterial bleeding from vessels in the underlying muscles. The small balls of lead first produce large, deep bruises, which are broken open by subsequent blows. Finally, the skin of the back is hanging in long ribbons and the entire area is an unrecognizable mass of torn, bleeding tissue. When it is determined by the centurion in charge that the prisoner is near death, the beating is finally stopped.

(3) Before Jesus was even placed on the cross, He was half-dead.

b. After He was almost whipped to death, (Mt. 27:35) explains that Jesus was then crucified on a cross.

(1) When Jesus was crucified, He was laid on two pieces of wood that were spread out to look like a cross. Then, the legionnaire presumable drove four wrought-iron nails through the wrists and feet of Jesus.

(2) Death by crucifixion developed into one of the world's most disgraceful and cruel methods of torture. Cicero called it "the most cruel and hideous of tortures. Flavius Josephus, the Jewish historian, who was an advisor to Titus during the siege of Jerusalem, had observed many crucifixions and called them "the most wretched deaths."

(3) After Jesus was nailed to the wood, He spent 6 horrifying hours in the hot, blistering sun hanging on the cross until finally He died.

3. Knowing what Jesus went through, how could anyone say that He did not actually die.

ILLUSTRATION:

A woman once wrote to a well-known radio preacher these words:

"Our preacher said that on Easter Jesus just swooned on the cross and that the disciples nursed him back to health. What do you think? The preacher replied, "Dear Sister, beat your preacher with a leather whip for thirty-nine heavy strokes. Nail him to a cross. Hang him in the sun for six hours. Embalm him. Put him in an airless tomb for three days. Then see what happens."

---

4. Jesus actually died on that cross and was buried in Joseph's Tomb.

> The Bible teaches that "Jesus breathed His last" (Mk. 15:37); "He gave up His spirit" (Mt. 27:50).

5. Further, Pilate was so sure that Jesus was dead, that he made sure himself before he gave Jesus' body to Joseph of Arimathea for burial.

6. Brethren, we can have rock solid faith that Jesus actually died on the cross.

B. SOME CRITICS ARGUE THAT THE RESURRECTION WAS A HOAX BY SUGGESTING THAT SOMEONE STOLE THE BODY OF JESUS.

1. Some say that the Roman or Jewish authorities removed the body of Jesus.

2. If that were the case, don't you think that on the day of Pentecost, when the Church was established, the Roman or Jewish authorities would have produced the body of Jesus in order to disprove the claims of Christianity.

3. Some say that Jesus' disciples stole the body.

The question that I have is how could they have accomplished this?

(1) The Bible says in (Mt. 27:62-66), that Pilate had a guard to secure the tomb.

(2) We must understand that a Roman guard was not a one, two, or three man force. A Roman guard was a 4 to 16 man security force. The 16 men in a square of 4 on each side were supposed to be able to protect 36 yards against an entire battalion and hold it. Normally, what they did was this: 4 men were placed immediately in front of what they were to protect. The other 12 were asleep in a semi-circle in front of them with their heads pointing in.

(3) These guys were well trained and took their jobs very seriously. In fact, Roman guards were immediately put to death if they ever left their night watch, or fell asleep.

4. There is no way that Jesus' disciples stole His body away from the well-trained and well-alert Roman guards.

C. SOME CRITICS ARGUE THAT THE RESURRECTION WAS A HOAX BY SUGGESTING THAT THE WOMEN WENT TO THE WRONG TOMB WHILE IT WAS YET DARK AND THAT, SEEING IT EMPTY, THEY REPORTED THAT JESUS HAD RISEN.

1. If they went to the wrong tomb, why didn't the authorities go to the right tomb, produce the body of Jesus, and disprove the disciples' claim?

2. Why is it that Peter later made the same so called "mistake" in broad daylight.

"Then Simon Peter, who was behind him, arrived and went into the tomb. He saw the strips of linen lying there..." (Jn. 20:6).

(1) How is it that both the women and Peter saw the empty grave clothes, if they were at the wrong tomb?

3. The reason why all of these theories are wrong and without merit, is because Jesus was resurrected from the dead.

4. The Bible teaches that after Jesus was raised from the dead, He appeared to over 500 different people at many different times throughout a 40-day period.

5. The only conclusion that we can come up with is that God raised Jesus from the dead. Here is the only theory we can trust in:

"For what I received I passed on to you as of first importance: that Christ died for our sins according to the Scriptures, that He was buried, that He was raised on the third day according to the Scriptures, and that He appeared to Peter, and then to the Twelve. After that, He appeared to more than five hundred of the brothers at the same time, most of whom are still living, though some have fallen asleep. Then He appeared to

James, then to all the apostles, and last of all He appeared to me also, as to one abnormally born" (1 Cor. 15:3-8).

6. By sharing the resurrection account with you, I hope that our faith has increased and that we have gained a better understanding of the events of the resurrection and how God's game plan was executed perfectly.

II. SECOND, HOW CAN WE BENEFIT FROM THE RESURRECTION OF JESUS?

A. SINCE JESUS WAS RESURRECTED FROM THE DEAD, WE CAN ALSO BE RESURRECTED FROM SPIRITUAL DEATH IN ORDER TO LIVE A NEW LIFE HERE AND NOW.

ILLUSTRATION:

Last year, I saw the movie, "Dead Man Walking." At the end of the movie, as Sean Penn was being transported to the electric chair, one of the guards yelled out, Dead Man Walking.

1. What caught my attention was even though he was still physically alive, the guard recognized him as a dead man.

2. Ironically, the Bible teaches the same thing. You can be alive physically, but spiritually dead. (Eph. 2:1, 2) "As for you, you were dead in your transgressions and sins, in which you used to live when you followed the ways of this world."

3. Most people are not aware of this, but unless a person believes in Jesus Christ; repents of their sins; confesses faith in Jesus; are baptized for the forgiveness of sins; and are living faithful lives in Christ; they are spiritually dead. They are "dead men walking."

4. However, the good news is that since Jesus was resurrected from the dead, we can be raised to a new life here and now. "Or don't you know that all of us who were baptized into Christ Jesus were baptized into His death? We were therefore buried with Him through baptism into death in order that, just as Christ was raised from the dead through the glory of the Father, we too may live a new life" (Rom. 6:3-4).

5. When we are baptized, meaning immersed in water, we are burying our dead sinful lives. When we come up out of the watery grave, we are given a new life. Our sins are done away with. We are literally raised from the dead!

6. Jesus came to give us life and have it more abundantly (Jn. 10:10). If you would like a new life and new beginning, through Jesus' death and resurrection, you can be raised from spiritual death this morning.

B. SINCE JESUS WAS RESURRECTED FROM THE DEAD, WE TOO CAN BE RESURRECTED AND LIVE FOREVER IN HEAVEN.

"God raised the Lord from the dead, and He will raise us also" (1 Cor. 6:14).

1. My friends, the good news is that we can escape death.

ILLUSTRATION:

Twenty-seven people are banking on the idea that modern science will someday find or engineer a fountain of youth. Those twenty-seven people, all deceased, are "patients" of the Alcor Life Extension Institute in Scottsdale, Arizona, where their bodies-or merely their heads!-have been frozen in liquid nitrogen at minus 320 degrees Fahrenheit awaiting the day when medical science discovers a way to make death and aging a thing of the past.

Ten of the patients paid $120,000 to have their entire body frozen. Seventeen of the patients paid $50,000 to have only their head frozen, hoping that molecular technology will one day be able to grow a whole new body from their head or its cell.

It sounds like science fiction, but it's called cryonics.

Thomas Donaldson, a fifty-year-old member of Alcor who hasn't yet taken advantage of its services, brushed aside the naysayers and explained to a reporter why he's willing to give cryonics a try: "for some strange reason, I like being alive....I don't want to die."

2. For those, like Donaldson, who like being alive, God has good news. Jesus Christ has risen from the dead with an eternal, resurrection body. He has conquered death. All of those who believe in Jesus and obey God's will, will someday also be raised from the dead with an eternal resurrection body. Jesus, not cryonics, is the only sure hope of eternal life.

Jesus said to her, "I am the resurrection and the life. He who believes in me will live, even though he dies; and whoever lives and believes in me will never die" (Jn. 11:25-26).

CONCLUSION:

1. In closing, many people have a hard time believing that salvation is obtained by believing in a man who was convicted as a criminal, and executed on a cross.

2. But the truth is that Jesus died on the cross to take care of our sins and was raised from the dead. Through God's perfect plan, through God's perfect strategy, which looks foolish to some people, we have become victorious--we have become winners.

3. The world thinks that we as Christians are running in the wrong direction...headed for the wrong end zone. But we are running in the right direction. We are headed for the right end zone.

4. My friends, God's wonderful game plan is for us to give our lives to His son Jesus Christ. This morning, if you would like to be a part of God's winning team, then please come down front and devote your life to the Lord. Come now as we stand and sing.

A FISH OUT OF WATER

Jonah 4:1, *But it displeased Jonah exceedingly, and he was very angry.*

JONAH buys a ticket at Joppa to go westward to Tarsus rather than to Nineveh.

He was going 800 miles in a westerly direction instead of the 300 miles in the easterly direction.

800 years later Peter had a similar dilemma at Joppa. "Take my message to Cornelius"

Don't call what I call unclean.

I see third problems with Jonah.

I. HE WAS OUT OF TOUCH WITH HIS SURROUNDINGS.

'ARISE GO, AND CRY."

Three times in 48 verses and 1328 words God tells him to **Wake up!!!.....ARISE AND GO!!**

When you are not doing right you will always be moving but in the wrong direction.

He may have been a minor prophet in the mind of theologians because of volume of verses but in the mind of God due to its intensity it is a major concern.

It is the only minor prophet Jesus ever quoted.

Bertrand Russell....Atheist

When you stand before God and find he really existed what will you say. He said, "I will say you did not give me enough evidence."

Romans: Man's problem is not the absence of evidence but the suppression of evidence.

Are we out of touch with the storm that is razing outside.

I fly a lot. But I have never learned to feel comfortable. I am convinced that God is spoken to at 35K feet more than at any other level.

Especially if you hear...We are having technical difficulties....prepare for an emergency landing....get in the brace position. Take hold of your ankles. Put head between knees and breath normally....Have you noticed the names...terminals...final approach. It seems no one is asleep at a time like this.

There is a storm all around us but we pretend to be asleep.

Connecticut woman...."I paid for filth and I didn't get what I paid for.

ADIRONIM JUDSON

He attended Rhode Island College in Providence. His roommate was a very intellect you man who believe was the same as his until leaving college.

One night many years later Adironim Judson was weary and tired and stopped at a hotel to sleep...he was put next to the room of a razing man who kept him awake until about 2 a.m. The next morning he inquired about the loud scream of the man. He learned the man had died. Then the hotel keeper said he did not understand the man's terrible death because he had been an honor student at R. I. college...His name was Jacob Ames...this had been his roommate...\Death....Hell....

He went to India but was kicked out....went to Burma and lost his wife and some of his children to disease. Married a second time and lost her to death...married a third time and was imprisoned in Burma...His wife visited him often in the prison...while he was attempting to complete the bible in Burmese while was translated the bible into Thai.

Because he was dying he was put on a ship back to USA.

Outside his home in Mauldin, Mass a stone contains the following:

The Rev. Adironim Judson...Born Aug. 19, 1788 Died April 12, 1850

Mauldin his birthplace

The ocean his sculpture.

Converted Burma with his bible, His monument.

His record is on high.

Prisoner Charlie Peace....Preacher was reading about hell...."If I believe half of what you are reading about I would craw across England over glass to warn everyone."

II. OUT OF TOUCH WITH HIS MESSAGE.

II Kings 5

Elijah had perform 8 blessings...Elisha wanted a double portion

No one ever was healed from leprosy until Naaman was healed by Elisha command to dip in river 7 times.

Where were you?....Nowhere in particular...

I am a father of two boys and when I would asked them, "Where were you? And they would answer nowhere in particular. I knew it was absolutely necessary that I would find out where they were in general.

GAHAZI....you have lied ...you followed Naaman and took the thing from him...Because He was healed of Leprosy you now will have his...

He lived surrounded by truth...but never applied it to his life.

Do you come to church surrounded by truth but never letting in sink into your life.

Scottish David Hume...Was seen with his raincoat placed tightly over himself was asked where he was going. I'm going to hear a preacher named George Whitfield preach.

You don't believe what he is preaching do you? No! but George Whitfield does. and I want to hear a man who does.

III...THE ONLY THING JONAH WAS IN TOUCH WITH WAS HIS COMFORT.

I admit that sometimes I have make my appointments to where I wanted to go. For such I have repented often..

Let me make an example by a potent story from one of the greatest missionary who has ever lived....David Livingstone.

As early as 9 years of age he had said..."Make me a missionary where you want me to go. Send me anywhere just go with me.

He married Martha Moffett...They lost their children and she her health. Finally they agreed she had to go back to her homeland for her health...The time passed until it was passed 5 years before they saw each other again. As they embraced at the seaport she pushed him back to look at him...she said a burned face which had not be prepared for the hot sun of Africa...A eye that had been punctured by a branch...The limp of a shoulder that had been mutilated by the attack of a lions attack and a walk that have shown a crippling.

But even with the prestige of the elite of Scotland, David Livingstone told his wife he still had the "burning in my heart for the 1,000 of villages untouched with the gospel."

They mutually agree he should return and she would follow later some years later.

Shortly after her return she contacts the same disease again dies. A bystander overheard him while was kneeing at her grave side say, "My Jesus, My King, My all, I again consecrate my life to thee, I will not value anything I process. Or in any thing I do except in relationship to thy kingdom and service.

He returns to his village and discovers his medicine had been taken. He cries out in a rare human prayer of preservation. You promised to take care of me...At which time he lifts his head to watch the approach of a white man...The man said, "I am Henry M. Stanley...An Atheist so don't bother me by trying to convert me...And I have brought medicine for you that had been sent from another.

David Livingstone did not once try to convert the man but Henry Stanley 4 months later was converted to the Christian faith because of the works of a man....He later writes a 2 vol. biography of one of the greatest missionaries of all times.

David Livingstone was found extremely tired by an attendant Tuma. He went to his chair and said "Wanna, Wanna' to see him slump dead in his chair.

Tuma carried him for 1500 miles through jungles, over rivers for 9 months to where he could ship his body back to England but not before he had cut out the heart and buried it in Africa.

David Livingstone died exactly like he tried to live.

1. In touch with his surroundings.

2. In touch with his message.

3. Out of touch with his own comfort.

The problems out there is not moral it is spiritual...

Are you willing to give up some of your comfort to do his will?

THE WONDER OF HIS CHURCH

PSALMS 78:54 "And He brought them to the border of His Sanctuary...which His right hand purchased."

The following words appear in the Holy Scriptures accordingly:

Church	77
Assembly	49
Sanctuary	137
Congregation	364
Learning	42
Language	22
Love	280
Destruction	32
Teach	108
Precept	5

One Holy Church of God appears
Throughout every age and race,
Unwashed by the lapse of years
Unchanged by changing place
-----Samuel Longfellow

INTRODUCTION: Accustomed as we are to criticizing the church, we need to remind ourselves that God's people are precious to Him.

As important as our private worship is, it must be balanced by congregational worship.

I. THE CHURCH IS ONE

I dislike terms like "invisible" "visible" Church

I dislike the term "Independent"

The visible church today has a mixture of "good and bad", "wheat and tares"

But, with all its spots and wrinkles, the church is still the Body of Christ in this world, the worshipping community that seeks to, "proclaim the praise of Him who called them out of darkness into His marvelous light." I Peter 2:9

The wonder of the church is not that we are a Perfect people, but a Purchased people, "redeemed with the "precious blood of Christ, as a lamb without blemish and without spot." I Peter 1:19

In spite of our defilement and division we are still "a chosen generation, a royal priesthood, nation, His own special people." I Peter 2:9

ILLUSTRATION: THE GREAT DIVIDE (YOHO NAT. PARK)

All visible churches are not created equal. There are some congregations whose doctrine and practice are so unbiblical that the faithful believer would not want to be identified with them. But we must be careful to "judge nothing before the time" I Cor. 4:5

Only God sees truth about each assembly.

The church at Smyrna thought it was bankrupt, but Jesus said it was rich.
The church at Laodicea thought it was rich but Jesus said it was "wretched, miserable, poor, blind and naked." Rev. 2:9, 3:17
John Calvin came to the conclusion that the "distinguishing mark of the church" are the preaching of God's Word and observing of the sacraments, or ordinances.

II. THE CHURCH IS ORGANIZED

It is both an organism and an organization and we dare not separate them.
A. An organism not organized will die.
God's church is organized and advises everything be "done in decency and in order." I Cor. 14:40.
B. Too much emphasis on organization produces an institution but too little will produce chaos.
The believers at Corinth grieved the spirit by disorder.
But the saints in Thessalonica were in danger of quenching the Spirit by over emphasis on order...WE NEED BALANCE.

<u>III. THE CHURCH IS ACTIVE</u>

IF WE ARE ACTIVE WE MUST <u>CONGREGATE</u> (364 times)
Exodus 40:26

Alter – witness
Laver – wash
Washed – whole

<u>As we congregate we are a part of a permanent union with Jesus.</u>

No other meetings can say that.

We are a distinct union.

"There is neither Jew nor Greek, there is neither slave or free, there is neither male nor female; for you are all one in Christ Jesus." Gal. 3:28. This is a miracle.

<u>We congregate because Jesus Christ is alive and coming again.</u>

- We meet on the Lord 's Day, the day of resurrection.
- Old creation – 6 days and rested.
- New creation – (The church) Jesus Christ finished His work on the cross, rested on seventh day as a completion of the old creation AND AROSE ON THE FIRST DAY OF THE WEEK.

Every time a church assembles on the Lord's day to worship, WE BARE WITNESS THAT Jesus is alive.

"Not forsaking the assembling of ourselves together, as the manner of some, but exhorting one another, and so much the more as you see the day approaching." Heb. 10:25

TO BE ACTIVE WE MUST <u>CELEBRATE</u>

We do something together-planned or spontaneous.

The heart of celebration is that we lift our hearts to God and express to Him our love and thanksgiving.

"Oh come, let us sing to the Lord! Let us shout joyfully to the rock of our salvation. Let us come before His presence with thanksgiving; let us shout to Him with Psalms " Psalms 95:10

"It shall be a Sabbath of rest…from even unto even, ye shall celebrate your Sabbath." Lev. 23:32

Just about everything the assembled church does can be classified as celebration:

Singing
Giving thanks
Sharing in offering
Encouraging one another
Reading and hearing God's Word

Platform – centered
Participant -- centered

IN OUR ACTION WE MUST COMMERMORATE

At TABLE we remember His Death
Resurrection
Coming again: Sure
Sudden
Silent
Selected
Satisfying

IN TESTIMONY

The Christian year commemorates the great events of sacred history.

Lord's birth
Baptism
Death
Resurrection
Coming of Holy Spirit after ascension

TO ARTICULATE WE MUST LEARN TO COMMUNICATE

PRAISE

Singing
Preaching

PROCLAIMATION

True worship involves witness:
To God.
To the church.
To the lost world.

MY AUTHORITY COMES WHEN I CONSECRATE (14 times, all O.T.)

ATTENDANCE at worship indicates we have consecrated our: (a) time to the Lord.

SHARING OUR OFFERING says we consecrate: (a) our means to the Lord.

OUR TALENTS AND GIFT given to Him means we consecrate ourselves for: (a) the Lord's use.

"HERE AM I, LORD! SEND ME!"

PRAYER BECOMES SERIOUS AS I COMTEMPLATE

There are times I must see what God is saying to me. "Let the words of my mouth and the mediation of my heart be acceptable in your sight, O Lord, my strength and my redeemer." Psalms 19:14.

Mission
Message
Ministry
Motivation
Direction
Devotion
Destiny

We have lost the Wonder of the church by allowing it to become boring and routine.

We must enter the congregation with that sense of awe that God has privileged us, even us, to be a part of His church.

"Who am I, O Lord God? And what is my house, that you have brought me this far?" I Sam. 7:18

- Sometimes I go to church as one of His SHEEP desperately needing the care of the Shepherd. "We are His people and the sheep of His pasture" Psalm 100:3.
- Sometimes as a member of the Body seeking energy I need for the ministry, or seeking to minister to others in the body.
- Sometimes I worship as a soldier in His army, wounded from the battles of the previous week.
- Sometimes I simply love Him as a part of His bride, and experience the inner joy and satisfaction that spiritual love can give.

I recall with shame that I criticized "sentimental Christianity" but have learned that my emotions are a part of worship, otherwise a part of me is not yielded to the Lord.

REVIEWING THE PRESENT

INTRODUCTION: Tonight I feel awesome being placed between a President Emeritus and a Preacher A-merited, since I was always a Pupil de-merited!

I feel much like the puffed up student selected by a group of professors to be taught all they knew about the flood. After weeks of intense teaching and training they were ready to send them to lecture to others. Noticing his conceitedness and haughty spirit felt he needed deflated before he left decided to tell him the following, "We have taught you all we know. You have the combined knowledge of those of us who have been your mentors. you know more than anyone we know about the flood. However, we feel you should know that where you will be speaking tomorrow at your first lecture you will have a very special guest we haven't even met. Noah will be there!"

I feel much the same way as I view the countless mentors, teacher, and leaders who grace this 50th Golden Anniversary.

My subject **"REVIEWING THE PRESENT"** is greatly influenced by a survey mailed to pastors in every conference of our National Association. Seventy-seven responses were received from this mailing representing 25 states and Canada. It represented large and small churches, city and rural, north and south, east and west. All responses were from pastors with a combined ministry of 1,681 years of service. The average age was 45 with the youngest being 27 and the oldest 67. They averaged beginning to preach at age 24 and oddly enough, while all pastors were selected at random from the national directory, the academic background averaged 4 years of college with 61 having attended college and 16 not having that privilege. The least educated had completed the 6th grade and the highest attained was 7 years of college. (Perhaps college men are more accustomed to surveys the reason for their greater response). Sixty (60) were full-time with 17 others supplementing their income. Of the respondents 57 said their church was growing and 20 said no. The average membership of their churches was 179 with the largest having 1,350 members and the smallest 20. They averaged 133 in attendance. Forty-six (46) said the attitude of their people toward church growth was average to good but 12 classified their churches attitude as excellent. Nineteen was poor to average.

Probably the most referred to item centered around leadership as being our key problem from Pastor, Membership, and routing itself to our National. Most pastors felt deficient in themselves and were seeking help from a national leadership they felt weak and divided without common goals.

Raymond C. Ortlund in his book, LET THE CHURCH BE THE CHURCH, tells of a pilot who announced over his intercom system, "Ladies and gentlemen, I have good news and bad news. The good news in that we have a tailwind and are making excellent time. The bad news is that our compass is broken and we have no idea where we are going."

There is a story in THE LAST HURRAH that illustrates my concern. The mayor of Boston is watching a parade. He says, "There go the people. I am their leader. I must follow them."

Since no one rises higher than leadership takes us, I feel it helpful that we look at the men the Master chose and how He developed leadership. How could Christ take 12 of the most changeable men and move the world. How could Jesus who knows all things make such a mistake in choosing such men of diversity?

May I suggest from the beginning that these were His best friends. And while we are concerned about being his friend we forget these were His whom He had called to train. They, like us, broke His heart many times as He sought to make them leaders.

Most of you probably cannot name all twelve of these men but they appear in the Bible in four different places

as an entire group. (Matthew 10:2-5; Mark 3:16-19; Luke 6:14-16; and Acts 1:13).

Matthew 10:2-5

Now the names of the twelve apostles are these; The first, Simon, who is called Peter, and Andrew his brother; James the son of Zebedee, and John his brother; [3] Philip, and Bartholomew; Thomas, and Matthew the publican; James the son of Alphaeus, and Lebbaeus, whose surname was Thaddaeus; [4] Simon the Canaanite, and Judas Iscariot, who also betrayed him. [5] These twelve Jesus sent forth, and commanded them, saying, Go not into the way of the Gentiles, and into any city of the Samaritans enter ye not:

Mark 3:16-19

And Simon he surnamed Peter; [17] And James the son of Zebedee, and John the brother of James; and he surnamed them Boanerges, which is, The sons of thunder: [18] And Andrew, and Philip, and Bartholomew, and Matthew, and Thomas, and James the son of Alphaeus, and Thaddaeus, and Simon the Canaanite, [19] And Judas Iscariot, which also betrayed him: and they went into a house.

Luke 6:14-16

Simon, (whom he also named Peter,) and Andrew his brother, James and John, Philip and Bartholomew, [15] Matthew and Thomas, James the son of Alphaeus, and Simon called Zelotes, [16] And Judas the brother of James, and Judas Iscariot, which also was the traitor.

Acts 1:13

And when they were come in, they went up into an upper room, where abode both Peter, and James, and John, and Andrew, Philip, and Thomas, Bartholomew, and Matthew, James the son of Alphaeus, and Simon Zelotes, and Judas the brother of James.

Please note that in all four lists Simon Peter is always listed first. Judas always appears last in the lists except in Acts where he has already betrayed the Lord. Note the disciples appear in all four lists **in three groups of four.** It is interesting to note the same person appears first in each of the three groups. Peter in group one; Phillip in group two; James the Less in group three.

Matthew 10	**Mark 3**	**Luke 6**	**Acts 1**
Simon Peter	*Simon Peter*	*Simon Peter*	*Simon Peter*
Andrew	*James*	*Andrew*	*James*
James	*John*	*James*	*John*
John	*Andrew*	*John*	*Andrew*
Philip	*Philip*	*Philip*	*Philip*
Bartholomew	*Bartholomew*	*Bartholomew*	*Thomas*
Thomas	*Matthew*	*Matthew*	*Bartholomew*
Matthew	*Thomas*	*Thomas*	*Matthew*
James	*James*	*James*	*James*
Thaddaeus	*Thaddaeus*	*Simon*	*Simon*
Simon	*Simon*	*Thaddaeus*	*Thaddaeus*
Judas Iscariot	*Judas Iscariot*	*Judas Iscariot*	*Judas Iscariot*

They also must have had a partner as well. This is indicated from Mark 6:7 as they were sent out two by two. *"And he called unto him the twelve, and began to send them forth by two and two; and gave them power over unclean spirits;"*

Sometime in your study observe who ran around with whom.

I believe I can fairly classify these three groups thusly:

Group one: The Presenters - The Vocal Ones - Authoritarian Leaders

Group two: The Contenders - The Varied Ones – Automatic Leaders

Group three: The Pretenders - The Vacillating One's - Appointed Leaders

Matthew 9:35-10:7, *"And Jesus went about all the cities and villages, teaching in their synagogues, and preaching the gospel of the kingdom, and healing every sickness and every disease among the people. But when he saw the multitudes, he was moved with compassion on them, because they fainted, and were scattered abroad, as sheep having no shepherd. Then saith he unto his disciples, The harvest truly is plenteous, but the labourers are few; Pray ye therefore the Lord of the harvest, that he will send forth labourers into his harvest. And when he had called unto him his twelve disciples, he gave them power against unclean spirits, to cast them out, and to heal all manner of sickness and all manner of disease. Now the names of the twelve apostles are these; The first, Simon, who is called Peter, and*

Andrew his brother; James the Son of Zebedee, and John his brother; Philip, and Bartholomew; Thomas, and Matthew the publican; James the son of Alphaeus, and Lebbaeus, whose surname was Thaddasus; Simon the Canaanite, and Judas Iscariot, who also betrayed him. These twelve Jesus sent forth, and commanded them, saying, Go not into the way of the Gentiles, and into any city of the Samaritans enter ye not; But go rather to the lost sheep of the house of Israel. And as ye go, preach, saying, The kingdom of heaven is at hand."

I. THE PRESENTERS - THE VOCAL ONES - AUTHORITARIAN LEADERS

A. SIMON PETER - THE OUTFRONT ONE

1. TESTED BY SPIRITUAL INVENTORY

Simon Peter - The task oriented leader. The text called him the first Simon. Not first by order of calling but rather the up-front, out-front man. The Greek word "Protos" is used. The same word is used in I Timothy 4:15, *"This is a faithful saying and worthy of all acceptation, that Christ Jesus came into the world to save sinners; of whom I am chief."*

Simon Peter. We know more about him than most all the other disciples. Next to the name of Jesus, Peter appears more than any other in the gospels. Nobody speaks as often as Peter and nobody is spoken to by the Lord as often as Peter. He is reproved by the Lord. No one acknowledges the Lordship of Christ as boldly as Peter, yet no one so boldly denied it as Peter.

He has 3 unusual characteristics:

a. Inquisitive. Peter asks more questions in the Gospels than all the other disciples combined.

E.g. (1) How often should I forgive? (Matthew 18:21).

"Then came Peter to him, and said, Lord, how oft shall my brother sin against me, and I forgive him? till seven times?"

(2) What reward will we get if we follow? (Matthew 19:27)

"Then answered Peter and said unto him, Behold, we have forsaken all, and followed thee; what shall we have therefore?"

(3) What about the fig tree that has withered? (Mark 11:21).

"And Peter calling to remembrance saith unto him, Master, behold, the fig tree which thou cursedst is withered away."

(4) What about the meaning of the need? (Mark 13:3).

"And as he sat upon the Mount of Olives over against the temple, Peter and James and John and Andrew asked him privately,"

b. Initiative. Peter not only asked questions but he was always the one who answered.

(1) When Jesus asked, *"Who touched me?"* (Luke 8:45) Peter answered.

(2) When Jesus asked, *"Who say ye that I am?"* (Matthew 16:15-16)
Peter answered.

(3) When Jesus asked, *"Will you also go away..."* (John 6:67) Peter said, *"To whom shall we go...you have the word of eternal life."*

c. **Involved.** Leaders are always in the middle of everything.

(1) Matthew 14:29. Peter jumped out of the boat and walked on the water. We criticize him for lack of faith but six others didn't have enough to even jump in.

(2) Peter denied Christ 3 times, but none of the others were nearby.
Earlier the men *"left all and followed Him"* but now they *"forsook Him and fled."*

(3) After the resurrection, John stood at the entrance of the tomb, but Peter rushed right in.

2. TAINTED BY SECULAR IDENTIFICATION

In John 1:42 Jesus at His first meeting of Simon said, *"Thou art Simon the son of Jona: Thou shalt be called Cephas, which is by interpretation, a stone."*

Simon was the name used when he was referred to by SECULAR identification.

(1) The house of Simon (Mark 1:29).

(2) Simon's wife's mother (Mark 1:30; Luke 4:38).

(3) Simon's boat (Luke 5:3).

(4) Simon's fishing partners (Luke 5:10).

(5) Simon's house (Luke 4:38, Acts 10:17).

When Jesus reprimanded him for SIN he was also called Simon.

(1) Luke 5:4-5, *"He said unto Simon, launch out into the deep, and let down your nets for a draught, and Simon answering said unto him, Master, we have toiled all the night, and have taken nothing. Nevertheless at thy word I will let down the net."* He is saying, This is ridiculous! We are the professionals. He is just a carpenter, O well. Luke 5:8... *"Depart from me; for I am a sinful man, O Lord."*

(2) Three times Jesus asked him, *"Simon, son of Jonah, lovest thou me?"*

(3) When Jesus builds him up, He calls him Peter.

3. TAUGHT BY SPIRITUAL INSISTENCE

Vocal leaders often pay dearly. Simon Peter did. You cannot know the impetuous, changeable Simon until you read his two little epistles in the back of the new Testament. Then you will see "The stone."

Vocal leaders would do well to study the life of Simon Peter's inconsistency.

B. ANDREW - THE MANLY ONE

1. THE TESTIFIER BECAUSE OF SPIRITUAL INCREASE

Andrew, whose name means *"manly"* never broke into the inner circle. Only once is he ever listed with the other three in a group and that is in Mark 13:3 when they sat upon the Mount Olives and asked Jesus, *"Tell us when shall these things be: and what shall be the sign when all these things shall be fulfilled?"*

Andrew was never as out front or forward as his brother.

(By the way, how would you always like to be referred to as someone's brother?)

All but one time Andrew is referred to as Simon Peter's brother.) In fact, he is not mentioned in any detail in the first three gospels (his calling, etc.), but in the Gospel of John he is mentioned in three distinct instances and in each he is doing the same thing. He was bringing people to Jesus.

a. John 1:40-42a He brought Peter to Christ.

b. John 6:8-9 He brought the little boy with fish and loaves.

c. John 12:20-22 he brought the Greeks to Christ.

Thank God there dwells among our denomination men still interested in bringing men to Christ. Soul winners who remain unsung and whose churches are growing. However, we need to be careful that our pride of success does not lead us to:

2. A TEMPTATION DUE TO SATANIC INTERVENTION

C.S. Lewis said, "The Source of pride is comparison."

History reveals few great churches exists from times past and they are only a shadow of its greatness. Time is our greatest enemy.

You may have a great church today and you should preach for its very soul for growth. But wait a little while. Give Satan time, your people time, your pride time. But be aware men die, movements fade, monuments fall, and only the message falters not. The flood of Hell cannot prevail upon the church of Jesus Christ.

Our greatest failure is to see things as:

Physical, Not Spiritual;
Earthly, Not Heavenly;
As Time, Not Eternal.

We Are Nearsighted, Out Of Focus;

Blind To Our Own Conceits;
Boastful In Our Own Capabilities;
And Burdened By Our Own Carelessness.

We have a tendency to:

i. View With Human Eyes And Dim The Eye Of Faith;
ii. To Weigh Things On The World's Scales, Not On Eternity's Balances;
iii. And To Obscure Present Realities With Pipedreams, Or Fantasies,
iv. Instead Of Giving Ourselves With Courage And Faith To Changing This World For Christ.

Remember, "History is His story and we have little regard for it."

C. JAMES - THE "HOT HEAD"

1. HE WAS TEMPERAMENTAL BY IMPLICATION

James' name always appears before his brother John in the gospels. Perhaps he was the elder or the one of stronger influence. James was fiery fellow evidence by Luke (9:51-56, *"And it came to pass, when the time was come that he should be received up, he steadfastly set his face to go to Jerusalem, And sent messengers before his face: and they went, and entered into a village of the Samaritans, to make ready for him. And they did not receive him, because his face was as though he would go to Jerusalem. And when his disciples James and John saw this, they said, Lord, wilt thou that we command fire to come down from heaven, and consume them, even as Elias did? But he turned, and rebuked them, and said, Ye know not what manner of spirit ye are of. For the Son of man is not come to destroy men's lives, but to save them. And they went to another village.*

"Let us pray that fire come from Heaven." I do not believe they would make good missionaries. Do you? Note Jesus rebuked them. In Mark 3:17, Jesus called *"...them Boanerges,* ---Sons of thunder."

2. HIS TEMPORARY MESSAGE DUE TO HIS IMPRISONMENT

The only place James appears without John is in Acts 12:1-4 when Herod subdues this zealous, aggressive, passionate, fervent man by taking his head. This occurs only 14 years after he wanted to know on which side of the Lord he would sit in the kingdom.

Acts 12:1-4 *"Now about that time Herod the king stretched forth his hands to vex certain of the church. [2] And he killed James the brother of John with the sword. [3] And because he saw it pleased the Jews, he proceeded further to take Peter also. (Then were the days of unleavened bread.) [4] And when he had apprehended him, he put him in prison, and delivered him to four quaternions of soldiers to keep him; intending after Easter to bring him forth to the people."*

D. JOHN - THE BELOVED DISCIPLE

1. THE TANTRUM OF INDICTMENT

The only time we find John alone in the Gospels is in Mark 9:38 and he is upset. *"Master, we saw one casting out devils in thy name, and he followed not us: and we forbade him, because he followeth not us."* At this time he was still sectarian, narrow-minded, unbending, intolerant.

My how we need to work on this. We are a diverse denomination. Born out of it. Still in it! Can't we be diverse without being divisive?

One respondent stated, "our problem is the vocal minority is unwilling to accept the diversity of our many."

More than half of the replies made mention of our:

- Lack of togetherness
- Division Intolerance of each other
- Lack of brotherly love
- Suspicion and jealousy
- Lack of doctrinal purity

While the other half expressed love and confidence in our leadership and denomination as a whole.

Dr. H. Stephen Shoemake of Louisville, relates a story he picked up. "A Texas rancher bought ten ranches and put them together into one big spread. His friend asked the name of the new ranch. The Texan replied, 'It's called the Circle Q, Rambling Brook, Double Bar, Broken Circle, Crooked Creek, Golden Horseshoe, Lazy B, Bent Arrow, Sleepy T, Triple O Ranch.' 'Wow!' the friend replied, 'I bet you have a lot of cattle.'

'Not many survive the branding.'

There is a temptation for us to "brand" each other negatively. But too much branding -- the Texan admitted-- can reduce the herd."

Dear friend if we are to exist, an honest effort of cooperation must prevail at all levels and must be made by every preacher and layperson.

- Defiance and rebellion have no place in the ranks of Godly men. An attitude and spirit of animosity, suspicion, and pride will finally destroy a preacher.
- Cooperation enhances unity, to which I am committed.

In Matthew 20:20-24 please note the self-interest of James and John in desiring to sit one on each side of the Lord. Note also they sent their mother to do the job of asking Christ but further find in verse 24 the other ten disciples *"Were moved with indignation against the two brethren."* *"Then came to him the mother of Zebedee's children with her sons, worshipping him, and desiring a certain thing of him. [21] And he said unto her, What wilt thou? She saith unto him, Grant that these my two sons may sit, the one on thy right hand, and the other on the left, in thy kingdom. [22] But Jesus answered and said, Ye know not what ye ask. Are ye able to drink of the cup that I shall drink of, and to be baptized with the baptism that I am baptized with? They say unto him, We are able. [23] And he saith unto them, Ye shall drink indeed of my cup, and be baptized with the baptism that I am baptized with: but to sit on my right hand, and on my left, is not mine to give, but it shall be given to them for whom it is prepared of my Father. [24] And when the ten heard it, they were moved with indignation against the two brethren."*

We are at a crossroads and we need to take a lesson from John as we find him becoming the:

2. TRUTH PRESENTER FROM SPIRITUAL IMPROVEMENT

Two words characterize John's later life and teaching: one is love and the other is witness. He uses the word **LOVE more than eighty (80) times** and the word **WITNESS in some form almost seventy (70) times.**

He becomes a real truth seeker. He was also borne out of the same zeal, passion and strength as was his brother James. He, like us had to work on loving his brothers.

One phrase stands out from the mature John. *"My little children, love one another."*

It is not what you are that is important, but what you are willing to become.

May we learn to:

- Respect the person
- Resist pride
- Restore piety
- Re-examine our priority
- Refine by prayer
- Reform by practice

We come now to:

II. THE CONTENDERS - THE VARIED ONES -- THE AUTOMATIC LEADERS

This type of leader is approachable. One should learn credibility is earned, not demanded.

A. PHILIP (MEANS LOVER OF HORSES)

He was the skeptical, pessimistic, and analytical one. But the Lord uses men like this as well.

In fact, he is always first in group number two. Our churches and conferences are full of this type person.

Men of caution, visionless often, but sometimes it is simply that they want to count the cost.

1. FINDING HIS POTENTIAL

The first three gospels don't tell us anything about Philip. But John's gospel mentions him four times.

- a. John 1:43-46. Where he is called to follow the Lord and where he leads Nathaniel to Christ.
- b. John 6:5-7. Where he was singled out by Christ relative to buying food for the 5,000. His response to Christ was, *"We couldn't get 200 pennyworth from the whole crowd."* What a shame to respond thusly when Jesus in verse 6 states why, *"And this He said to test him; for He knew himself what He would do."*

Philip was a materialist, methodical and mechanical. The type who would take out his pocket calculator and say, "We can't afford it!"

- He appears In the same three chapters as does Andrew but lacks the faith.
- He represents in part our stewardship program. We need to be unified in our denominational giving. We have never taught our people to give Biblically. A host of pastors don't tithe and multitudes of our members have never received the blessings or joy of giving.

Our churches have been selfish. Therefore, due to the lack of outside giving has resulted in the withholding of God's blessing in every area of our denomination.

We need a Stewardship Commission to educate us. Or a stronger emphasis in our publications and colleges toward giving beyond our own local church to a total ministry.

Nearly every strong, virile denomination that is growing today has taught their people the value and blessing of unified giving.

Out of the top 10 giving states, 6 give through the unified co-op plan. An analyses revealed the fastest growing giving states were in this program. While it does not pay all the bills, those states involved were also the fastest growing toward quotas set by the departments and in e establishing strong state and local agencies.

In the spirit of fairness however, it should be mentioned that other strong giving states exists who have not adopted this program.
Have we been against this program because of its author? The argument remains, but those who oppose enjoy spending the benefits none the less.

c. John 12:20-22. Here Philip brings the Greeks that come to him to Andrew who take them to Christ.

d. John 14:8 *"Lord show us the Father."*

Many men like Philip have walked, led, sat where Christ is, but have yet to fully see the Father or Son. He followed Christ for over three years, but it is conceivable he represents so many yet today. However, he did have a seeking heart in the midst of his insecurity.

B. BARTHOLOMEW (NATHANAEL)

Only one place tells us anything about him aside from the four lists and that is in John 1:46-51 where he is called Nathanael. Let us note here:

1. THE FLAW BECAUSE OF PREJUDICE

He along with Philip, were students of the Scripture as noted in verse 45. But we see his sin when Nathanael was told about Jesus. He said, *"Can anything good come out of Nazareth?"*

In the recent survey it appeared many were saying, "Can anything good come out of Nashville?"

On a national level many sense:

- A lack of evangelistic thrust.
- Narrow scope for growth.
- Unwillingness to face the issues.
- Power struggle among departments.
- Leadership out of touch with the pastorate.
- Need new faces in old places.
- Place the Heavenly degree above the Nashville degree.
- Growth department catering just to large churches.

The more complimentary suggestions were:

- Need unity without uniformity.
- Return to Christian love.

- Rekindle the old paths.
- Gear toward the small church to help them.
- Speak to our needs.
- Prepare correspondence courses for leaders-preachers.
- Literature improvement.
- Prepare literature for churches for growth.
- National ministers retreat.

PREJUDICE IS AN UNCALLED FOR GENERALIZATION BASED ON FEELINGS OF SUPERIORITY.

Prejudice is ugly in any form. It was prejudice that kept the Pharisees from responding because he wasn't from Jerusalem. They said of the apostles in Acts 2:7, 4:13 that they were ignorant, unlearned, Galilean hayseeds. Acts 2:7 *"And they were all amazed and marvelled, saying one to another, Behold, are not all these which speak Galilaeans?* " Acts 4:13 *"Now when they saw the boldness of Peter and John, and perceived that they were unlearned and ignorant men, they marvelled; and they took knowledge of them, that they had been with Jesus."*

Prejudice is used by Satan to blind people.

However, I'm glad Nathanael's prejudice was not deep and we see,

2. HIS FAITH SEEN BY THE PHENOMENAL ONE

"Behold an Israelite indeed, in whom is no guile." Verse 47.

Thank God! That while prejudice exists among us, the tribe is dying.

Like, Nathanael our knowledge of the Word is causing us to be less judgmental.

May we be seekers of truth, not bound by prejudice, but honest, open, people of prayer.

Every child of God must one day stand before Christ to have his lifetime of service investigated.

Second Corinthians 5:10 states, *"We must all appear before the judgment seat of Christ; that every one may receive the things done in his body, according to that he hath done, whether it be good or bad."*

This judgment of believers is exclusively the responsibility of the Lord Jesus Christ. No mere mortal is capable of assuming the place of an omniscient, omnipotent God when it comes to judging men and movements. Finite human beings, regardless of their fundamental pedigree or position, are incapable of looking into another man's heart.

Only God can judge righteously. He said in Jeremiah 17:10, *"I the Lord search the heart, I try the reins, even to give every man according to his ways, and according to the fruit of his doings."*

This is why the Holy Spirit emphatically declares in Romans 14:4, 10-13: *"Who art thou that judgest another man's servant? to his own master he standeth or falleth. Yea, he shall be holden up: for God is able to make him stand...But why dost thou judge thy brother? or why dost thou set at nought thy brother? for we shall all stand before the judgment seat of Christ. For it is written, As I live, saith the Lord, every knee shall bow to me, and every tongue shall confess to God. So then every one of us shall give account of himself to God. Let us not therefore judge one another anymore: but judge this rather, that no man put a stumblingblock or an occasion to fall in his brother's way."*

We need to be careful about proclaiming and publishing the latest faults of brethren.

Remarks made against anyone are not worthy to be classified under the heading of 'defending the faith,' but rather as 'sowing discord among brothers,' a sin God adamantly hates (see Proverbs 6:16-19). *"These six things doth the Lord hate: yea, seven are an abomination unto him: [17] A proud look, a lying tongue, and hands that shed innocent blood, [18] A heart that deviseth wicked imaginations, feet that be swift in running to mischief, [19] A false witness that speaketh lies, and he that soweth discord among brethren."*

Until the Lord is allowed to correct this terrible sin through a Holy Spirit-empowered revival of genuine love, our movement will decline and eventually die.

A healthy body cannot exist without love.

C. MATTHEW (LEVI) - THE WORST ONE

The only picture we see of Matthew is found in three places (Matthew 9:9-13; Mark 2:14-17; Luke 5:27-32).

It is the same incident. <u>That of sitting at the seat of custom.</u> Note:

1. THE FAME FROM WHICH HE PROPELS

He was a tax collector. However, he was willing to leave it entirely. Being a publican was not easy. It was even worse when you know the scriptures of y our fathers but not permitted in the temple because you were a Publican. There were outcast. Remember the publican who sat afar off and said, *"God be merciful to me a sinner."*

The Jewish Talmud said, *"It is righteous to lie and steal from tax collectors."*

Matthew must have felt he was the worst one of the lot because he alone in the listings of the twelve gives his occupation as a publican. The publicans were hated and despised by the Jewish society.

Matthew in recording this is showing his genuine humility and expressing his sinful unworthiness.

While Matthew never speaks, never asks a question, never appears in another incident, his book is loaded with an appreciation for Christ.

2. THE FORGIVENESS HE PROPOSES

3. Matthew 9:9-13, *"And as Jesus passed forth from thence, he saw a man, named Matthew, sitting at the receipt of custom: and he saith unto him, Follow me. And he arose, and followed him. And it came to pass, as Jesus sat at meat in the house, behold, many publicans and sinners came and sat down with him and his disciples. And when the Pharisees saw it, they said unto his disciples, Why*

> *eateth your Master with publicans and sinners? But when Jesus heard that, he said unto them, They that be whole need not a physician, but they that are sick. But go ye and learn what that meaneth, I will have mercy, and not sacrifice: for I am not come to call the righteous, but sinners to repentance."*

The theme of Matthew's message can in part be summed up in this same chapter as he asks which is greater, *"to be saved from your sins or healed."*

This book, called the Book of the King of Kings to the Jews, perhaps is so noted due to his including more Old Testament quotes of the Law and History than all the other gospels combined.

May I draw your attention to the distance he comes in order to follow Christ.

There were two classes of Tax collectors: The Gabbai and Mokhes.

The Gabbai were the general collectors that collected property tax, income, poll tax, etc.

The Mokhes collected duty and tolls on everything. They were divided into two groups. The Great Mokhes who hired others to do the collecting as he faded from sight and the little Mokhes who were too greedy to hire anyone else.

Matthew is saying I was a little Mokhes. I came from the table. I was saved from the undermost to the uttermost.

He like another publican (Zacheaus) did something no one else did after their conversion. They gave a banquet for their Saviour.

D. THOMAS - NOT A DOUBTER

What do you think of when you think of Thomas? Doubter? If you do you believe wrong. I believe he got bad press. Let us look at:

1. HIS FAITH WE DESIRE TO REPROVE

In John 10:39 we find the account of where Jesus and the disciples had left Jerusalem because of the plot to take his life. But in John 11:14-16 the news of Lazarus's death is received and Jesus decides to return back to Bethany near Jerusalem. This caused a panic by the disciples except Thomas.

"Let us also go, that we may die with him." Verse 16b.

This is not characteristic of doubter/s but rather because he totally believed in Christ.

John 14:1-5 *"Let not your heart be troubled: ye believe in God, believe also in me. In my Father's house are many mansions: if it were not so, I would have told you. And if I go and prepare a place for you, I will come again, and receive you unto myself; that where I am, there ye may be also. And whither I go ye know, and the way ye know. Thomas saith unto him, Lord, we know not whither thou goest; and how can we know the way?"* Here he is saying, Lord don't you go somewhere we can't come. Thomas had a problem with separation. I don't like what I hear. You are going somewhere and we can't get there. We'll never find the place.

Jesus was crucified in John 19 and Thomas was destroyed. In John 20:24-29 we have the account of the disciples being gathered in the upper room after the crucifixion but Thomas was not there.

I knew it! He died and I didn't. I wanted to go with him and be where he is but he is gone.

He was depressed and had left the others who by the way were in the upper room "for fear."

Thomas was probably kicking every can in Jerusalem. He believed He was gone.

Before you label Thomas "the doubter" remember that none of the other disciples believed

Jesus had risen until they saw him.

We should see Thomas in the light of John 20:29, *"Thou hast believed."* Here we see:

2. HIS FIDELITY WE SHOULD REDUPLICATE

Our faith and trust falters and our denomination needs to return to a stronger and deeper commitment to the Christ of our salvation.

We must take a look at our faith in what He wants to do in and through us.

We need to:

a. Define our Purpose - that's Motive.
b. Discover our Potential - that's Measure.
c. Determine our Priorities - that's Manner.
d. Direct our Program - that's Message.

Remember the Lord builds His church with:

a. A Sanctified Preacher.
b. A Separated People.
c. A Salvaging Passion.
d. A Saturating Program.

I am a denominational person owing my conversion to this movement, but frankly I'm not sure God is a thrilled that there is a Free Will Baptist denomination as I am. But I am sure he is concerned about my indifference to the lost or my lack of reaching the lost here and around the world.

He is more concerned that people are saved than we continue as a denomination.

The reason any organization exists is to fulfill its preamble. If it wavers it has lost its reason to be. The responsibility is ours. We may:

a. Shirk it, because we are afraid to undertake it.
b. Shelve it, because we are anxious to defer it.
c. Shed it, because we are tired of hearing it.

Or,

a. Shoulder it, because we are ready to fulfill it.
b. Share it, and be wise in distributing it.

Men or every level who are known as leaders but whose pride robs of true repentance can create a dike holding back the needful revival for themselves and those they influence.

The streams of revival are held back when cold hearts continue to hold ill feelings. We will never experience revival and restitution:

- Until pastors and parishioners forgive each other.
- Until churches and conference forgive each other.
- Until states and leaders forgive each other.
- Until every organization can say, I forgive!

When all our people: from President to pastor; leader to layman; can practice Matthew 18:15. *"Moreover if thy brother shall trespass against thee, go and tell him his fault between thee and him alone: if he shall hear thee, thou hast gained thy brother."*

Then and only then will we move forward. Until we do, one must surely be fearful in saying, "let us go that we may die with him." How can He forgive us our trespasses when we don't. May the fountains of the Water of life, the Washing of regeneration once again flow and flood every member of our denomination.

III. THE PRETENDERS -- THE VACILLATING ONE'S -- APPOINTED LEADERS

This third group represents a segment of our movement and they are many.

In many ways our people are suffering from a lack of good leadership. A vast number of our membership have a mistrust of denominational affiliation due to misinformation. Communication falls rapidly from the National to the local church. Only about 8,000 receive Contact Magazine and maybe four times that amount receive *Mission-Grams* and *Heartbeat.* But this is far short of reaching the more than 200,000 members.

We have 22 states publishing 22 different publications, but going to only about 42,000 people. Each defining or carrying the denominational message with their own bias.

A great transition exists today with a stronger emphasis being given to the local and state ministries. In fact, 22 states now have their own State Executive or Promotional Secretaries where the state and national programs are being promoted and with time a stronger program from the local conference to national convention will exit. Until then, national organizations would better their own programs by coordinating with these state leaders.

We now have 28 regular state conventions, 17 Free Will Baptist Bible Institutes in 10 states, 75 Christian schools in 22 states, 13 or so full-time evangelists, 4 colleges geographically centered across the United States, 9 National Boards and Commissions made up of 68 men and women, with 110 Foreign missionaries in 9 countries and 122 Home missionaries in 28 states and Canada, Mexico, Virgin Islands, and Puerto Rico. We also have 8 chaplains serving in the Armed services. In addition the National

Sunday School Department dedicated a new Spanish curriculum this year adding to its 1 million, 400 thousand yearly units of printed curriculum.

Our 1984 statistics reveals we had 210 district associations, 2,598 churches and 213,025 members.

With plenty of prayer, preparation and a positive approach we can reach into every area of our denomination like never before.

Now let us look at these four disciples who always appear in this group. Just like our mass of people of whom we know so little, these disciples are the ones of whom we know only a little.

A. JAMES - THE SON OF ALPHASUS

The only thing the Bible tells us about this disciple is his name. He never says a word nor is spoken to but he is still one of the twelve.

1. THE DESIGNATION HIS NAME PRESENTS

In Mark 15:40 he is called *"James the Less."* The Greek word used in this title is "mikros" which means little. However, while it basically means "small in stature."

Could it also mean "young in age" or "one of little influence?"

We may never know, but the Bible does tell us.

2. SOME DETAILS OF HIS PEDIGREE

a. Could Matthew have been his brother?

According to Mark 2:14 Levi (Matthew) was also a son of Alphasus.

b. Could Jesus be his cousin?

In John 19:25, *"Now there stood by the cross of Jesus His mother, and His mother's sister, Mary the wife of Clopas..."*

Can we assume that no mother would name two daughters Mary and that she was actually a sister-in-law of Mary? Also, Clopas is another form of the name Alphasus. Is it possible that Alphaesus as Joseph's brother making Christ and James cousins? To further substantiate this is Mark 15:40 where it refers to a Mary as *"The mother of James the Less."*

This James represents a vast multitude of our movement. There are thousands of people, mainly in leadership roles in churches and conferences, totally unknown outside his area. He is none the less their leader, and his influence, while little nationally or statewide, is followed locally. He is the overlooked person and is the person to be reached before the grassroots will ever be touched.

Be as it may, while not recognized outside his region, he like James will be recognized in Heaven. The Lord does use obscure, little, unknown, unsung men.

B. LEBBAEUS (JUDAS THADDAEUS)

1. THE DEFINITION OF HIS PERSONALITY

His name was Judas (Jehovah leads).

The names Lebbaeus and Thaddaeus may have been added at a later time to reflect his character.

Thaddaeus comes from the Hebrew root Thad. It carries with it the meaning of being a "breast-child." He may have been the youngest child. The baby of the family.

Lebbaeus comes from the Hebrew root Leb, which means "heart." A man of courage -- a heart-child.

2. THE DECLARATION OF HIS PRIORITIES

This man was also lost in obscurity but we find him one time in the scripture.

John 14:21-24, *"He that hath my commandments, and keepeth them, he it is that loveth will manifest myself to him. Judas saith unto him, not Iscariot, Lord, how is it that thou wilt manifest thyself unto us, and not unto the world? Jesus answered and said unto him, If a man love me, he will keep my words: and my Father will love him, and we will come unto him, and make our abode with him. He that loveth me not keepeth not my sayings: and the word which ye hear is not mine, but the Father's which sent me."*

Jesus' answer simply put would be, "I can tell who loves me by the way they obey me. And only those who truly love me and obey me will I manifest myself to. The only people who will be able to perceive me are the ones who love me."

In other words, manifestation is limited to reception.

I believe ones dedication will be determined by:

a. The Master you serve.
b. The Message you share.
c. The Morals you Sanction.
d. The Manners you show.

It was Bob Jones, Sr. who said, <u>"The level of Responsibility is determined by the level of opportunity."</u>

- A leadership with integrity does not wait to see what the trends are, or what is popular.
- The true leader sets the trends and rallies the people, even when the cause is unpopular.
- How can the church remain silent when millions of unborn infants are being slaughtered?
- How can the church remain silent when we are having an epidemic of divorce and are witnessing the breakdown of the family?
- How can the church remain silent when racism has become sophisticated and hidden in political philosophy?
- How can the church remain silent when there are those who are demanding that homosexuality be recognized as a valid Christian life style.
- How can the church remain silent when our culture is drowning in a sea of alcohol? Where are the Carry Nations of our time?

C. SIMON -- THE ZEALOT (JEALOUS FOR THE LAW)

In Matthew and Mark, Simon is identified as <u>"Simon the Canaanite."</u>

Luke and Acts record him as "Simon, called Zelotes." The Greek word used for Zelotes has the same meaning as the Hebrew root quana where the transliteration Kananaios is used.

The meaning of the words being "to be jealous."

Simon may have been identified with a party of Judaism known as the Zealots. His was one of the four dominant groups within Judaism! The Pharisees, Sadducees, Essenes, and the Zealots.

1. THE DOCTRINE HE PRESENTED

The zealots were the most fervent, passionate, patriots of Judaism. Probably born out of the Maccabean period where Judas Maccabaeus led a revolt against Greek influences on the Jewish nation and religion. The intensity of the Zealot philosophy is seen in I Maccabees 2:50, *"Be ye zealous for the law and give your lives for the covenant."*

In New Testament times the Zealots fled to Masada after the destruction of Jerusalem led by a man named Eleazar. Here 960 zealots committed suicide rather than be taken by the hated Roman enemy according to Josephus, the Jewish historian (Wars of the Jews, book VII, Chapters VIII and IX).

2. HIS DETERMINATION ABOVE HIS PARTNER

I believe that Simon's partner was Judas Iscariot as Jesus sent out the disciples two by two (Mark 6:7).

But Simon continued to believe and was transformed. Judas however fell short of the Mark.

I believe as Free Will Baptists we have failed to indoctrinate our people. We give up more people to denominations with a foreign biblical doctrine than we receive from others. I have observed many people join our churches across our denomination as I visit churches. Many were made members without having knowledge of our beliefs. Most didn't have the opportunity to even reject our covenant because it wasn't read to them. Many will never be taught our doctrine. That which made us what we are was a common belief and an abiding conviction about apostasy, feet washing, free communion, and local church autonomy separating us from other denominations and their beliefs. These beliefs have been the chains that bind us together.

Many movements that are growing today are not side stepping doctrinal emphasis, but make it the center of their preaching along with salvation. The stress is on conversion, baptism, joining the local church, and living separated lives. Until we do this our losses will continue.

D. JUDAS ISCARIOT

The name Judas was a common one. Simply the Greek from of Judah-the land of God's people. Some say its root meaning is "Jehovah praised" but others "one who is the object of praise."

In any case it is sad that it was given to the one who rejects his Lord.

Iscariot basically comes from a combination of the Hebrew term Ish, which means "man," and Kerioth, the name of a town. He was the *"Man of Kerioth."* He was Judas of Kerioth.

In fact, he was the only disciple not from Galilee since Kerioth was in Judea near Hebron south of Jerusalem. Since he was not one of the acquaintances or brothers could it be he was never accepted as one of the group? However, he continues even from the beginning.

Remember Jesus demanded total commitment as early as John 6:66, *"From that time many of His disciples sent back, and walked no more with him."* Many left but the twelve stayed. Could he have been motivated by selfish purposes? What type of relationship did he have with Christ?

Psalm 41:9, *"Yea, mine own familiar friend in whom I trusted who did eat of my bread, hath lifted up his heel against me."*

Psalm 55:12-14, 20b-21, *"For it was not an enemy that reproached me; then I could have born it. Neither was it he that hated me that did magnify himself against me; then I would have hid myself from him: But it was thou, a man mine equal, my guide, and mine acquaintance. We took sweet counsel together, and walked unto the house of God in company...............he hath broken his covenant. The words of his mouth were smoother than butter, but war was in his heart: his words were softer than oil, yet were they drawn swords."*

Zechariah 11:12-13, *"And I said unto them, if ye think good, give me my price; and if not, forbear. So they weighed for my price thirty pieces of silver. And the Lord said unto me, cast it unto the potter: a goodly price that I was prised at of them. And I took the thirty pieces of silver, and cast them to the potter in the house of the Lord."*

John 17:12, *"While I was with them in the world, I kept them in the name: those that thou gavest me I have kept, and one of them is lost, but the son of perdition; that the scripture might be fulfilled."*

Luke 22:21-22, *"But behold, the hand of him that betrayed me is with me on the table. And truly the Son of man goeth, as it was determined: but woe unto that man by whom he is betrayed!"*

1. HIS DESIRES DURING THE PRETENSE

Judas never has a word to say until he complains about the money that Mary wasted in anointing Jesus' feet. This is the first time he speaks in the entire biblical record.

John 12:3-6, *"Then took Mary a pound of ointment of spikenard, very costly, and anointed the feet of Jesus, and wiped his feet with her hair: and the house was filled with the odour of the ointment. Then saith one of his disciples, Judas Iscariot, Simon's son, which should betray him, Why was not this ointment sold for three hundred pence, and given to the poor? This he said, not that he cared for the poor; but because he was a thief, and had the bag, and bare what was put therein."*

REMEMBER THE SAME SUN THAT MELTS THE WAX HARDENS THE CLAY.

Was he the hypocrite of hypocrites? No one even suspected him. Outwardly, Judas appeared not to have a defective character. In fact, he was not even considered a betrayer right up to the last supper by his peers. When he left the upper room the other disciples thought he had only gone out to buy more food.

Judas had heard the same lessons as the other disciples.

a. The unjust steward (Luke 16:11-13).
b. The wedding garment (Matthew 22:11-14).
c. Lessons about money (Matthew 23:1-12).
d. Jesus even forewarned by saying in John 6:70b, *"One of you is a devil."* Even John 13:21, *"Verily, verily, I say unto you that one of you shall betray me."*

2. THE DISTANCE HE PLANNED

John 13:10b-11, 18-19, 21-29, *"He that is washed need not save to wash his feet, but is clean every whit: and ye are clean, but not all. For he knew who should betray him; therefore, said he, ye are not all clean....I speak not of you all: I know whom I have chosen: but that the scripture may be fulfilled, he that eateth bread with me hath lifted up his heel against me. Now I tell you before it come, that, when it is come to pass, ye may believe that I am he.....When Jesus had thus said, he was troubled in spirit, and testified, and said, Verily, verily, I say unto you , that one of you shall betray me. Then the disciples looked one on another, doubting of whom he spake. Now there was leaning on Jesus' bosom one of his disciples, whom Jesus loved. Simon Peter therefore beckoned to him, that he should ask who it should be of whom he spake. He then lying on Jesus' breast saith unto him, Lord, who is it? Jesus answered, He it is, to whom I shall give a sop, when I have dipped it. And when he had dipped the sop, he gave it to Judas Iscariot, the son of Simon. And after the sop Satan entered into him. Then said Jesus unto him, that thou doest, do quickly. Now no man at the table knew for what intent he spake this unto him. For some of them thought, because Judas had the bag, that Jesus had said unto him, buy those things that we have need of against the feast; or, that he should give something to the poor."*

Matthew26:16, *"And from that time he sought opportunity to betray him."*

Mark 14:11, *"And when they heard it, they were glad, and promised to give him money. And he sought how he might conveniently betray him."*

Luke 22:6, *"And he promised, and sought opportunity to betray him unto them in the absence of the multitude."*

John 18:2-4, *"And Judas also, which betrayed him, knew the place: for Jesus ofttimes resorted thither with his disciples. Judas then, having received a band of men and officers from the chief priests and Pharisees, cometh thither with lanterns and torches and weapons. Jesus therefore, knowing all things that should come upon him, went forth, and said unto them, Whom seek ye?"*

Matthew 27:3,5, *"Then Judas, which had betrayed him, when he saw that he was condemned, repented himself, and brought again the thirty pieces of silver to the chief priests and elders. And he cast down the pieces of silver in the temple, and departed, and sent and hanged himself."*

Acts 1:18, *"Now this man purchased a field with the reward of iniquity; and falling headlong, he burst asunder in the midst, and all his bowels gushed out."*

Matthew 27:6-7, *"And the chief priests took the silver pieces, and said, it is not lawful for to put them into the treasury, because it is the price of blood. And they took counsel, and bought with them the potter's field, to bury strangers in."*

Acts 1:15-26, *"And in those days Peter stood up in the midst of the disciples, and said, (the number of names together were about a hundred and twenty.) Men and brethren, this scripture must needs have been fulfilled, which the Holy Ghost by the mouth of David spake before concerning Judas, which was guide to them that took Jesus. For he was numbered with us, and had obtained part of this ministry. Now this man purchased a field with the reward of iniquity; and falling headlong, he burst asunder in the midst, and all his bowels gushed out. And it was known unto all the dwellers at Jerusalem; insomuch as that field is called in their proper tongue, Aceldama, that is to say, The field of blood. For it is written in the book of Psalms, Let his habitation be desolate, and let no man dwell therein: and his bishoprick let another take. Wherefore of these men which have companied with us all the time that the Lord Jesus went in and out among us. Beginning from the baptism of John unto that same day that he was taken up from us, must one be ordained to be a witness with us of his resurrection. And they appointed two, Joseph called Barabbas, who was surnamed Justus, and Matthias. And they prayed, and said, Thou, Lord, which knowest the hearts of all men, shew whether of these two thou hast chosen. That he may take part of this ministry and apostleship, from which Judas by transgression fell, that he might go to his own place. And they gave forth their lots; and the lot fell upon Matthias; and he was numbered with the eleven apostles."*

Psalms 69:25-28, *"Let their habitation be desolate; and let thy wrathful anger take hold of them. Let their habitation be desolate; and let none dwell in their tents. For they persecute him who thou hast smitten; and they talk to the grief of those whom thou hast wounded. Add iniquity unto their iniquity: and let them not come into thy righteousness. Let them be blotted out of the book of the living, and not be written with the righteous."*

Judas represents those of our movement falling short of God's purpose for his life.

today we have a faltering family unit, pastors and laymen alike are falling speedily into the separation of the family. Many of our great and good men, preachers of the gospel, have become victims of divorce.

Others are open prey for Satan's attack. It is advisable to remember Philip Brooks saying, *"If God called you to preach, never stoop to be a king."*

We need like never before a Family Life Commission and a strong emphasis on the Christian family in every area of our movement. It cannot be left to the clergy for they are hurting to and the church needs the message

Conclusion: Teaching our people is one of our failings. Another is legalism. We seem to have the idea no better way exists than our own. With this type of attitude, our churches will cease to meet the needs of a changing society. I think most of our churches have reached the height of their growth. I don't think it's impossible for them to grow; I think it's improbable that they will. Therefore, if our denomination is to grow it will take new churches being organized. It will take men dedicated to the cause of growing a church for the cause of Christ.

Since there is a constant upward mobility involved in society as a whole, we need to strengthen, maintain, nourish, and develop our existing churches. We must open new churches for our children who are leaving our rural areas and going to cities, graduating from universities, becoming involved in industry. We cannot forget to serve every area of our changing society.

On a national level, we need to capitalize on what God had allowed us to have as denominational resources--our Bible college, Sunday school department, executive office, and mission departments. These departments are not mini-denominations with only their desire in mind. But we are one denomination with many organizations that need to remember we are one.

Our colleges need to produce men who are dedicated to our cause who believe we are a total denomination without prejudice to the uneducated or non-Bible college trained minister. Our mission departments should gear up in fulfilling the design of their organization with a cooperating spirit as the body advances. Our publications should foster unity in the body, and our curriculum press prepare material designed for edification

All working together will provide the impetus we need for a unity which will produce growth.

The first Austrian to ever win a gold medal did so in the 1968 Olympics with a hand gun. He hit the bull's eye 100 times for a perfect score. Upon his return to Austria he was highly honored by his countrymen and sent out to inspire the youth. After the fanfare died he returned to his job. Only a short time later he lost his left hand in the machine at the plant he worked. Remembering the past he became quite discouraged. In fact, very hard to live with. One evening he came in pushing aside his wife and entered the bedroom where in the chest he found a pistol. His wife, knowing his deep despair, fell to her knees, paralyzed as she cried, "Oh, no." From the home he left crossing over the hillside. SHE SUDDENLY HEARD A BANG. Jumping to her feet she hastened and just as she hastened to the sound, just as she peered over the hillside, suddenly another bang. bang. bang. bang.

In 1972 he won his second gold medal by hitting the bull's eye 99 out of 100 times.

He, while discouraged and despaired and crippled faltered, never lost his dream.

May we as Free Will Baptists not lose sight of our goal, our dream.

THE WORD OF ENCOURAGEMENT

Millions of people around the globe watched with tears in their eyes and cheers in their throats as Derek Redmond crossed the finish line.

Redmond was the British runner in the 400-meter race at this week's summer Olympic games in Barcelona. He was running with all his heart when he heard a pop in his right hamstring and he clutched his leg. He fell to one knee, his face contorted with pain. Then he rose in unbearable agony, and started toward the finish line, hopping on one leg and dragging the other behind him.

Moments later, an American won the race, but after the cheering died down, people noticed Redmond, his body exploding in pain, hobbling toward the finish line.

Suddenly, Redmond's father jumped from the stands

Together they hobbled on, step by excruciating step, until they staggered across the line. The crowd went wild, cheering more for the British runner than they had for the American who had won the race.

He was a boy with a father who had come along side to help.

Jesus said, "I will ask the Father and He will send the Holy

Spirit, who is the Comforter," or, as it might be, "the Counselor." The Greek word is *parakleetos --"one who comes alongside to help."*

As we "run with patience the race before us"

<u>That's the job and the role of the Holy Spirit for the Christian.</u>

Well, the primary way the Holy Spirit strengthens and encourages us is with Scripture.

According to Hebrews 12, this is the "Word of Encouragement."

And look at Romans 15:4--*For everything that was written in the past was written to teach us, so that through endurance and the encouragement of the Scriptures we might have hope.*

And look at chapter 1: *I long to see you so that I may impart to you some spiritual gift to make you strong -- that is, that you and I may be mutually encouraged by each other's faith.*

Paul was referring here to the encouragement of his spoken word, but the truth applies to the written word as well. The letter Paul wrote to the Romans is perhaps the most powerfully encouraging document the world has ever received.

<u>All roads in Scripture lead to Romans.</u> It's the book that explains the doctrine of the Gospel more methodically and

systematically than any other book in the Bible. And that's why whenever, wherever the book of Romans is preached, souls are saved, revival occurs, and the people of God are encouraged.

In the summer of A.D. 386, about 300 years after Paul wrote this letter in Gaius's Corinthian villa, another Roman was in a friend's garden, weeping and broken. He had lived a wildlife, full of immortal sexual adventures and polluted by alcohol. He was profane and pagan. He was brilliant, teaching rhetoric at the university; but he was confused and ruined. As he sat weeping in his friend's garden, he heard a child nearby singing the words of a song: *Take up and read; take up and read.*

He picked up the book beside him and began reading it. It was the book or Romans. Within one sentence, he was converted to Jesus Christ, and his life was changed forever. His name was Aurelius Augustinus, and he became one of the greatest minds and most profound leaders in Church history--Saint Augustine.

Saint Augustine helped shape and guide the church as the Roman Empire collapsed around him. Within Augustine's lifetime, the Visigoths invaded Rome, and shortly thereafter, Rome fell, the Western Roman empire ended, and darkness enveloped the world.

The quality and integrity of the papacy gradually decreased until it reached its lowest point during the pontificates of Pope Alexander VI and Pope Leo X. Pope Alexander VI was famous for becoming intimate with women whose marriages he had just performed. He would bring in the wedding couple, perform their marriage, dismiss the husband, and lead the bride from the chapel into his bedroom.

That's not the worst of it. His banquets were nothing bur orgies.

Pope Alexander fell in love with his own daughter, committed incest, and impregnated her with a son. The pope was at the same time the boy's father and grandfather! This man was supposed to be the greatest example of Christ in the world, but you see how degraded the earth had become.

But during the days of Alexander, a boy was growing up in a German home, the son of peasants. As a young man, he entered the priesthood. He traveled from Germany to Rome to see the Vatican and to worship the Papacy; but when he saw the corruption and the immorality and the evil of it all, he was shattered. He returned to Germany and started studying the book of Romans. Day after day and night, he pondered the book of Romans, especially chapter 1, verse 17: *For in the Gospel a righteousness that is by faith from first to last, just as it is written: The righteous will live by faith.*

Suddenly, the light burst through those pages and Luther rediscovered the doctrine of justification by grace through faith. He started preaching and teaching the truth of Romans, and the Protestant Reformation swept across Europe and eventually around the world.

The Christian world was revived and renewed because of this book that Paul wrote during his three months in the guest quarters of his wealthy friend in Corinth.

At the very same time that Luther was pouring over the book of Romans in Germany, another young man was studying it in England. He was studying Romans in the Greek, because there was no English translation of the Bible in existence. This young man, William Tyndale, dreamed of translating the Word of God into the English language, and he set himself to the task. Tyndale replied: *"If God spare me, ere many years I will cause the boy that drives the plough to know more of the Scripture than you do."*

Tyndale translated the New Testament into English, but no one in England dared print it. He fled to the continent looking for a printer, only to find himself hunted like an escaped serial killer. He finally printed his English New Testament, but in the process he was captured by British agents, imprisoned, tried, publicly strangled with the iron collar, and his corpse was burned at the stake.

It eventually became the basis for the King James translation of the bible in 1611.

But after Luther and Tyndale, as the years passed, the Protestant world, too, fell into lethargy and corruption. The lamp of the Gospel burned low. In England, there was very little zeal for the things of the Lord, and it looked as if Christianity would again perish from the earth.
Then another young man grew up in England. He read the King James Version of the Bible, and was moved enough by

it to leave Europe and sail to America as a missionary to the Indians of Georgia. But he wasn't really a Christian himself. He didn't know the Lord, and he returned to England broken and depressed.

One night John Wesley went to a little Gospel meeting in Aldersgate Street, London, and listened to someone reading from Luther's commentary on Romans. Instantly he saw the light, he was converted, and, as he put it later, his heart was "strangely warmed." His ministry launched the Evangelical Revival of the eighteenth century.

It's incredible that some of the most significant moments in church history were pivoted by the book of Romans. All the roads in the Bible lead to Romans; and all the roads in Romans lead to the Savior. It's the book in the Bible that explains clearly and systematically the Gospel doctrine of justification by grace through faith. And it's the *Word of Encouragement*.

Still today, the book of Romans is changing lives. Col. Harland Sanders of Kentucky Fried Chicken fame.

The minister invited him to an evangelistic meeting, and that night Co. Sanders claimed the promise of Romans 10:9 -- that if we believe in our hearts and confess with our mouths that Christ Jesus is Lord, we shall be saved.

The apostle Paul was an inspired man when he wrote this Epistle.
Yet Paul, inspired as he was, frequently quoted from the Old Testament: Psalms - "As it is written, The reproaches of

them that reproached thee fell on me." One special reason for quoting from the Old Testament was, doubtless, to put honour upon it, for the Holy Spirit foresaw that there would be some, in these later days, who would speak of it disparagingly. Not so did our Lord Jesus Christ; not so did his apostles; no so did any by whom the Holy Ghost spake. The Old Testament is not to be regarded with one jot less of reverence and love than is the New Testament; they must remain bound together, for they are the one revelation of the mind and will of God; and woe be to the man who shall attempt to rend asunder that seamless garment of Holy Scripture.

There are some who speak of the Old Testament as if it were worn out; but, indeed, it has about it all the freshness, and the force, and the dew of its youth; and, in the additional light that the New Testament throws upon its histories, its prophecies, and its promises, it has gathered force rather than lost any, so that we, probably, can appreciate the Old Testament Scripture far more highly now, that we have the New Testament also than we could have done if we had not received both the early and the later revelations.

Some have supposed that the light of the New Testament is so bright that it quite eclipses the light of the Old Testament.

So, first, we will consider the patience of the Scriptures; secondly, the comfort of the Scriptures; and then, thirdly, though that may not be precisely according to the letter of the text, yet, I think, the hope of the Scriptures.

The first question in the Westminster catechism is, "What is the chief end of man?" This might be amplified as follows: What is the main purpose of life? What end are we to have in view in all of our living? What is to be the basis of all our thoughts and decisions? What are the principles for directing the course of our life?
The answer given in the catechism is: "Man's chief end is to glorify God and to enjoy Him forever."

Relationships: Matthew 5:44
"But I say unto you, Love your enemies, bless them that curse you, do good to them that hate you, and pray for them which despitefully use you, and persecute you; "

Romans 1:6-7
"Among whom are ye also the called of Jesus Christ: [7] To all that be in Rome, beloved of God, called to be saints: Grace to you and peace from God our Father, and the Lord Jesus Christ."

"Called to belong to Jesus Christ . . . to all God's loved . . . who are called to be saints." (Rom. 1:6, 7).

This like-mindedness must exist among brethren who are designated as strong and weak. The weak are not to criticize the strong for their liberties in Christ, and the strong are not to expel the weak from the church. Rather, the two groups are to live in oneness for mutual good and edification.
Believers are not to think in terms of being "a good Presbyterian," "a good Baptist," "a good Lutheran," "a good Methodist," "a good Roman Catholic," "a good Anglican," or

any other such category, but only in terms of being a good and faithful servant of the Lord Jesus Christ, and because of Him, good and faithful servants one of another.

This is what the Word of God means when it tells us to be "like-minded."

- It does not mean that all believers must agree on the manner and mode of Baptism,
- Or on the manner and mode of ordination,
- Or on the details of events connected with the second coming of Christ.
- It does mean that we are to agree on who Christ is, what He came to do, on the fact that He accomplished what He purposed to do, and that he is on the throne of the Father today in order to be Lord of the Church.
- If we can be in accord on these things, true harmony should then flow from our yieldedness to the Lord Jesus Christ, who certainly is seeking to draw all believers to Himself.

Now it is evident that we can never reach a true basis of accord until we have the mind of Christ. Literally, our text says, "that he might give you the same mind according to Christ."
Our text is not concerned with "the mind of Christ" in relation to doctrine, but with the attitude of Christ in relation to others.

Back in the twelfth chapter we had the exhortation, "Live in harmony with one another; do not be haughty, associate with the lowly." (12:16).
That is a plea for social harmony among believers. Our present text is a plea for harmony and tolerance among believers.

In Romans the Greek word (*phroneo*) is found ten times, and "like-minded" in our present text is the last occurrence (8:5, 12:3; 12:16; 14:6; 15:5).

WHAT PRICE HARMONY

When Christ's ministry began to take pre-eminence, John the Baptist said, "He must increase, but I must decrease" (John 3:30).

In fact, we are told, "In humility count others better than yourselves" (Phil. 2:3).

If we fail in this, we are actually elevating our carnality above someone else's carnality.

MAGNIFY THE LORD

Our text is not a profound philosophical definition of the glory of God. The Apostle Paul is telling us that when believers live in harmony with one another they give the outside world a better view of God. How terrible, then, when our disagreements give men the excuse to follow their own ways and to remain aloof from all groups of believers!

We are to glorify God. We are to magnify Him.

- The Greek word for *glory* is *doxa*. The doxology is the word of praise.
- The earliest meaning of *doxa* was opinion; if a man had straight opinions he was *orthodox*;
- if he had other opinions he was *heterodox*.
- If two opinions are not the same but each seems right, they form a *paradox*.

ONE MIND AND ONE VOICE

One of the great verses of the New Testament is the soul-rending revelation that, in regeneration, "We have the mind of Christ" (1 Cor. 2:16). "That you may with one mind and one mouth glorify God."

Years later Augustine wrote that everything hidden in the Old Testament was to be found open in the New Testament.

- Paul's purpose in this section of his epistle is to unite the two parties in mutual respect and love.
- The Jews had become "weak" because they were afraid that they might transgress some of the dietary laws of the Old Testament.
- The Gentile believers regarded these conscientious scruples with a rough intolerance that was far from the spirit of Christ.
- In quoting a Psalm of David and applying it to Christ, Paul showed the Jews that the Old Testament was much greater than they had ever conceived it to be, and he showed the Gentile believers that between the lines of the former revelation are great eternal principles.

First of all, we can deduce from this text that the Old Testament is not a compilation of the best in human thought about God.
Neither is the Bible the record of man groping after God, but God's revelation of Himself to man.
It is initiated by God for many purposes, one of which is revealed here.

HOPE
Our text leads us away from despair and past doubt into learning, patience, comfort, and on to our goal -- hope. It must be understood that *hope* in the Bible sense is not the same as *hope* in our modern civilization.

The young man is asked how he fared in his examination. He crosses his fingers and says, with a wry grimace, "I passed, I hope, I hope, I hope."

The girl who has never had a date may fill a cedar chest with linens for her future home, if and when she gets one; and the world calls this a "hope chest."

There is no thought of such uncertainty in the Bible word translated *hope*, for in the Christian hope there is all the strength and certainty of the Lord Jesus Christ." It is ultimate, final, and absolute.

"HEART EDUCATION"
First, the road to hope leads through learning. Our text says that all that God caused to be written in the past was

written for our learning, our instruction. We must understand that God is not speaking of mere mental knowledge, which may become like a hard blood clot that suddenly destroys life. The Lord Jesus has given us a remarkable thought on this aspect of learning. When He taught that He was the living Bread come down from Heaven, they murmured. He answered, "It is written in the prophets, 'And they shall all be taught by God.' Everyone who has heard and learned from the Father comes to me" (John 6:45).

A HOPE THAT BLESSES OTHERS

It is a certainty which possesses us now, and makes us like the Lord Jesus Christ in all our relationships.

LIFE THROUGH THE WORD

- Do not forget that it is impossible to find God apart from His Word.
- The Holy Spirit does not come to any soul independently if the Bible.
- He dwells in the hearts of those who trust in Christ.
- He leads us on from day to day, but He will never lead us without the Word, and He will always lead us into the deeper patience and comfort of the Scriptures.
- Flee any teaching that the Holy Spirit furnishes knowledge apart from the Word of God.

And just as the Holy Spirit teaches us only by the Word, so He can teach us from any part of the Word. Christ spoke well when He said, "Man shall not live by bread alone, but by *every* word that proceeds from the mouth of God" (Matt. 4:4).

Dozens of Old Testament stories are mentioned in the New Testament.

"By faith Abraham obeyed when he was called to go out to a place which he was to receive as an inheritance; and he went out, not knowing where he was to go" (Heb. 11:8).

If we had no other record than this we might think that Abraham heard the command of God, clicked his heels, saluted, and cried out, "Forward, March! One, two, three, four; one, two, three, four!" **Romans 15:1-8**

[1] We then that are strong ought to bear the infirmities of the weak, and not to please ourselves.
[2] Let every one of us please his neighbor for his good to edification.
[3] For even Christ pleased not himself; but, as it is written, The reproaches of them that reproached thee fell on me.
[4] For whatsoever things were written aforetime were written for our learning, that we through patience and comfort of the scriptures might have hope.
[5] Now the God of patience and consolation grant you to be likeminded one toward another according to Christ Jesus:
[6] That ye may with one mind and one mouth glorify God, even the Father of our Lord Jesus Christ.
[7] Wherefore receive ye one another, as Christ also received us to the glory of God.

I. Obligation (ver. 1). --"We, the strong ones, ought to keep on bearing the weaknesses of the powerless ones, and not to be wanting continually to please ourselves."

Christians are to bear, not merely to for bear; there must be patient submission and the endeavor to support the weakness of our brother by loving forethought and tenderness.

The keynote of the verse is in the word "ought," implying the consciousness of a profound obligation. Even the etymology of "we ought" is suggestive. It always means, "we owe it."

II. Edification (ver. 2).

-- The aim of each and every individual Christian should be to please his neighbor for good, with a view to building him up in the Christian faith and life. **This is the supreme law of brotherhood, and the Apostle practiced what he preached** (I Cor. ix. 19-22; x. 32, 33).

III. Imitation (ver. 3).

--For Christ also pleased not Himself." The Master did the very same thing as the Apostle here urges his fellow-Christians to do. This is the first reference to the example of Christ in the Epistle.

IV. Confirmation (ver. 3).

--"As it is written, the reproach of them that reproached thee fell on me." The Scripture foretold the action of the Messiah in this very respect (Psa. 1xix. 0). It is striking to observe that there are more references to Psa. 119. in the New Testament in relation to Christ than to any other, and this would seem to show that in many respects the Psalm is intended to express Messianic experiences.

V. Inspiration (ver. 4).
--the reason for quoting the Old Testament is now seen to be in the purpose of that book as a whole. It was written to uphold believers in their life of patient hope. They were to learn, and from learning to derive endurance and comfort, which in turn would lead to hope.

VI. Supplication (vers. 5, 6). --**From the Scriptures the Apostle turns to God Himself as the Source of endurance and comfort.** Wherever the Greek word here rendered "patience" is found we are to understand active endurance, not passive resignation. It suggests the presence, not the absence of difficulty, and attitude of determined, deliberate steadfastness under pressure.

- This grace comes from God through the Scriptures, and will in turn bring us and our fellow-Christians into unity, Christ being the standard: "according to Christ Jesus."
- Oneness with God will lead to oneness among brethren.
- When God is first the result will be unity.
- Not identity of union but harmony of feeling.
- It is to be observed that of the two unities emphasized by the Apostle in Ephesians iv., one is present and the other is future: "the unity of the Spirit" (ver. 3) we are to keep with all possible endeavor; but "the unity of faith and knowledge" (ver. 13) will not come yet, but will be reached someday (cf. Phil. iii. 15-17; iv. 2, 3).

VII. Application (ver. 7). --Now comes the closing exhortation and appeal to both parties. Each is to acknowledge and treat the other as Christians.

1. The Pattern of Christ's Example.
Twice in this brief passage is this truth taught. In His earthly life our Lord did not please Himself (ver. 3), and we are to "follow His steps."

In His heavenly life we are to be of one mind, "according to Christ Jesus" (ver. 5).

St. John's First Epistle lays great stress on Christ as our pattern. No less than **six times he uses the phrase**, "even as He."

- We are to "walk in the light, as He is in the light" (Ch. i. 7).
- We are to "walk, even as He walked" (Ch. ii. 6).
- We are to "purify ourselves, even as He is pure" (ch.iii.3).
- And we are to "love, as He gave us commandment" (Ch. Iii.23).

When St. Peter speaks of Christ "leaving us an example, that ye should follow His steps" (1 Pet. ii.21), he quickly refers to our Lord as the Sin Bearer, as the Life, and as the Shepherd and Bishop of our souls (verse. 24, 25).

2. The Power of Holy Scripture. Herein is another secret of power in the Christian life. Whatever grace is needed is found in Holy Scripture. It was intended for this very purpose, and it always accomplishes its end when properly used. **It contains truth because it is a Divine revelation.**

There is nothing in Christianity so potent for Christian living as a daily, definite, first-hand meditation of the Word of

God. It is as impossible to exaggerate its power, as it is impossible to over-estimate the loss that accrues when our Christian life is not supported, sustained, and guided day by day by this close contact with Holy Scripture.

3. The Provision of Prayer. As the Apostle turns from Scripture to the Source of Scripture, so we in our daily life must resolve everything into prayer. Prayer means power, because it links us to the Fount of power, God Himself.

Verse 5. *Now the God of patience and consolation grant you to be like minded one towards another, according to Jesus Christ.*

STEWARDSHIP IS LORDSHIP

Proverbs 3:5-10, *"Trust in the LORD with all your heart; and lean not unto your own understanding. In all your ways acknowledge him, and he shall direct your paths. Be not wise in your own eyes: fear the LORD, and depart from evil. It shall be health to your navel, and marrow to your bones. Honor the LORD with your substance, and with the first fruits of all your increase: So shall your barns be filled with plenty, and your presses shall burst out with new wine."*

"For as a man thinks within himself, so he is."- Proverbs 23:7

INTRODUCTION: Normally when we think of stewardship, we consider it merely as a matter of our giving of money to God through the church. While the giving of tithes and offerings is an important aspect of stewardship, it is secondary.

"Stewardship is the way I handle those things in my life that God has given me...The Management of my God-given resources for His glory & for the good of others..."

<u>Stewardship is a reflection of my relationship to my God and my Savior.</u> As I observe the truths contained in Proverbs 3, I see a pattern for stewardship that asserts loudly and clearly "Stewardship is Lordship!"

I. MY HEART – HIS HEART

<u>(Trust in the LORD with all your heart)</u>

A. At the heart of every true act of stewardship, every work of ministry, every acceptable act of worship is the heart, a heart close to God.

B. John 14:23 *"Jesus answered and said unto him, 'If a man love me, he will keep my words: and my Father will love him, and we will come unto him, and make our abode with him'."*

C. A French soldier who had served ably in Napoleon's army lay dying of a wound received in battle. As they probed his shattered ribs to find the fatal bullet he said, *"Dig a little deeper and you will find the emperor."* If we dug deeply enough, would we find Christ in our hearts? That's a question we all must ask ourselves. - Robert C. Shannon, 1000 Windows, (Cincinnati, Ohio: Standard Publishing Company, 1997).

D. As Sir Walter Raleigh was about to be executed, he was asked which way he preferred to lay his head on the block. He replied, "So the heart be right, it is no matter which way the head lies." [Robert C. Shannon, 1000 Windows, -(Cincinnati, Ohio: Standard Publishing Company, 1997).]

E. Proverbs 23:26 *"My son, give me thine heart, and let thine eyes observe my ways."*

F. Bill of $22.22 cents. Rutherford invited me to golf game.

II. MY MIND – HIS MIND

(lean not unto your own understanding)

A. Oswald Chambers (1874-19170, "Christian thinking is a rare and difficult thing; so many seem unaware that the first great commandment according to our Lord is, *"Thou shalt love the Lord thy God . . . with all thy mind."*

B. Proverbs 23:7 *"For as he thinks in his heart, so is he: Eat and drink, saith he to thee; but his heart is not with thee."*

C. 2 Corinthians 10:5 *"Casting down imaginations, and every high thing that exalts itself against the knowledge of God, and bringing into captivity every thought to the obedience of Christ;"*

D. Stewardship involves allowing God to work in us. Tozer said, "To do his gracious work God must have the intelligent cooperation of his people. If we would think God's thoughts, we must learn to think continually of God."

E. I Corinthians 2:16 *"For who hath known the mind of the Lord, that he may instruct him? But we have the mind of Christ."*

F. Philippians 2:5 "*Let this mind be in you, which was also in Christ Jesus:"*

G. Philippians 4:8 *"Finally, brethren, whatsoever things are true, whatsoever things are honest, whatsoever things are just, whatsoever things are pure, whatsoever things are lovely, whatsoever things are of good report; if there be any virtue, and if there be any praise, think on these things."*

III. MY WAYS – HIS WAYS

(In all your ways acknowledge him, and he shall direct your paths.)

A. Way – path or direction. Is the direction of your life consistent with the direction that God wants for your life?

B. Isaiah 55:8 *"For my thoughts are not your thoughts, neither are your ways my ways, saith the LORD."*

C. God instructed King David as recorded in 1 Kings 2:4 *"That ...if David's children would take heed to their way; to walk before God in truth with all their heart and with all their soul; he not fail have one of his descendants perpetually on the throne of Israel."* (Paraphrased)

D. Psalms 128:1 *"A Song of degrees. Blessed is every one that fears the LORD; that walks in his ways."*

E. There is peace, prosperity, and safety in being in the center of God's will and walking in His ways.

F. David Livingstone told how he was chased up a small tree and besieged by lions. He said the tree was so small that he was barely out of reach of the lions. He said they would stand on their back feet and roar and shake the little tree, and that he could feel the hot breath of the lions as they sought him. "But," he stated, "I had a good night and felt happier and safer in that little tree besieged by lions, in the jungles of Africa, in the will of God, than I would have been out of the will of God in England." There is one safe and happy place, and that is in the will of God. [William Moses Tidwell, "Pointed Illustrations."]

G. Haggai 1:5-7 *"Now therefore thus saith the LORD of hosts, 'Consider your ways. Ye have sown much, and bring in little; ye eat, but ye have not enough; ye drink, but ye are not filled with drink. Ye clothe you, but there is none warm; and he that earns wages earns wages to put it into a bag with holes.' Thus saith the LORD of hosts, 'Consider your ways.'"*

H. Proverbs 16:7 *"When a man's ways please the LORD, he makes even his enemies to be at peace with him."*

IV. MY CLEANLINESS – HIS CLEANLINESS

(Be not wise in your own eyes: fear the LORD, and depart from evil.)

A. Ecclesiastes 12:13 *"Let us hear the conclusion of the whole matter: Fear God, and keep his commandments: for this is the whole duty of man."*

B. Romans 12:1-2 *"I beseech you therefore, brethren, by the mercies of God, that ye present your bodies a living sacrifice, holy, acceptable unto God, which is your reasonable service.*

[2] And be not conformed to this world: but be ye transformed by the renewing of your mind, that ye may prove what is that good, and acceptable, and perfect, will of God."

C. Purity in the heart produces power in the life – power to properly live for and serve God.

D. 2 Timothy 2:19-21 *"Nevertheless the foundation of God stands sure, having this seal, The Lord knows them that are his. And, Let everyone that names the name of Christ depart from iniquity. [20] But in a great house there are not only vessels of gold and of silver, but also of wood and of earth; and some to honor, and some to dishonor. [21] If a man therefore purge himself from these, he shall be a vessel unto honor, sanctified, and meet for the master's use, and prepared unto every good work."*

E. God uses clean vessels.

F. The essence of true holiness is conformity to the nature and will of God. –Samuel Lucas (1818-1868)

V. MY POSSESSIONS – HIS POSSESSIONS

(Honor the LORD with your substance, and with the first fruits of all your increase)

A. Adolphe Monod (1800-1856)

"There is no portion of our time that is our time, and the rest God's; there is no portion of money that is our money, and the rest God's money.

It is all his; he made it all, gives it all, and he has simply trusted it to us for his service. A servant has two purses, the master's and his own, but we have only one."

B. We are to use everything as if it belongs to God. The truth is it does! You and I are merely his stewards.

C. As John Wesley said, "When the Possessor of heaven and earth brought you into being and placed you in this world, He placed you here not as an owner but as a steward. As such He entrusted you for a season with goods of various kinds--but the sole property of these still rests in Him, nor can ever be alienated from Him. As you are not your own but His, such is likewise all you enjoy."

D. Malachi 3:7-10 *"Even from the days of your fathers ye are gone away from mine ordinances, and have not kept them. Return unto me, and I will return unto you, saith the LORD of hosts. But ye said, Wherein shall we return? [8] Will a man rob God? Yet ye have robbed me. But ye say, wherein have we robbed thee? In tithes and offerings. [9] Ye are cursed with a curse: for ye have robbed me, even this whole nation. [10] Bring ye all the tithes into the storehouse, that there may be meat in mine house, and prove me now herewith, saith the LORD of hosts, if I will not open you the windows of heaven, and pour you out a blessing, that there shall not be room enough to receive it."*

E. 1 Corinthians 16:1-2 "*Now concerning the collection for the saints, as I have given order to the churches of Galatia, even so do ye. Upon the first day of the week let every one of you lay by him in store, as God hath prospered him, that there be no gatherings when I come."*

F. "A handful of people went on a mission trip to Eastern Europe. Upon returning, they said that they were really impressed with the dedication of the Christians in Eastern Europe. Christians there don't have very much, but they believe they should tithe. They think that's God's standard. But the government of the country they were in is repressive, and they are allowed to give only 2.5 percent of their income to charitable organizations. They're trying to minimize the opportunity for any anti-government organization. So the Christians in that country are searching for loopholes in the law, so that they'll be able to give 10 percent. These believers have less, and they're looking for a way to give 10 percent. We have more, and we're free to give as we please. In fact, we get a tax break by doing so, and we're looking for loopholes in the Scripture to avoid doing it. What an indictment." – adapted from Bob Russell, "Take the Risk," Preaching Today, Tape No. 143.

G. Some get upset when pastors talk about money. Jesus talked much about money. Sixteen of the thirty-eight parables were concerned with how to handle money and possessions. In the Gospels, an amazing one out of ten verses (288 in all) deals directly with the subject of money. The Bible offers 500 verses on prayer, less than 500 verses on faith, but more than 2,000 verses on money and possessions.

H. Luke 12:34 "*For where your treasure is, there will your heart be also.*"

I. Some say, dedicate the heart and the money will follow; but our Lord put it the other way around. "Where your treasure is, there will your heart be also."

If your treasure is dedicated, your heart will be dedicated. If your treasure is not, your heart simply is not. It is as plain as that.

VI. HIS PROMISE – MY BLESSING

(So shall your barns be filled with plenty, and your presses shall burst out with new wine.)

CONCLUSION: 1 Corinthians 4:2 declares, *"Moreover it is required in stewards that a man be found faithful."* Every one of us will give an accounting to Christ for our stewardship of those things, which He has entrusted to us. If your heart his heart? Is your mind His mind? Are your ways His way? Is your cleanliness His cleanliness? Are your possessions His possessions? On that accounting day will Christ say to you, *"Well done, good and faithful servant; thou hast been faithful over a few things, I will make thee ruler over many things: enter thou into the joy of thy Lord."(Matthew25:23)*

The Vision-- He wants to give us a vision.

The Provision--God has already provided the needed resources! He never gives vision without provision. He anticipates the need and meets it in advance. As someone once said, "God's work done in God's way will always have God's resources."

Here is the great principle: The Lord places in our hands the resources of the world. Deuteronomy 8:18 says: "But remember the LORD your God, for it is He who gives you the ability to produce wealth…. " "All we have is His and it all comes from Him. The Bible teaches that the earth is the Lord's and everything in it"(Psalm 24:1).

He gives and gives and gives to His people. Why? Why do we have the money we have? Some of you may have stocks and bonds. Why does God give us those things? The mutual funds? The saving accounts? The houses and lands and possessions?

The Decision-- Each of us has a decision to make, and we should make it without coercion or human pressure, for I believe God will prompt us. But we must have willing hearts.

Recently I came across one of the most famous stories in fund-raising history. It occurred in the year 1912. Dr. Russell H. Conwell, pastor of Grace Baptist Church in Philadelphia, had a little girl in Sunday School named Hattie May Wiatt who lived nearby. The Sunday School was very crowded, and one day Dr. Conwell told her that he would love to have buildings large enough to allow everyone to attend who wanted to.

Later, Hattie May became ill and died. Rev. Conwell was asked to preach the funeral, and the girl's mother told him that Hattie May had been saving her money to help build a bigger church. The mother gave him the little girl's purse, and it contained fifty-seven cents (which represented a large amount for a poor little girl in those days). Rev. Conwell took those coins to the bank and exchanged them for fifty-seven pennies which he put on display and "sold." With the proceeds, a nearby house was purchased and the property was converted into a children's wing for the church. Inspired by Hattie's story, more money came in, and out of her fifty-seven cents eventually came the buildings for the buildings of Temple Baptist Church in Philadelphia, Temple University, and Good Samaritan Hospital.

In the book Tortured for Christ, Richard Wurmbrand tells of his many years in and out of miserable Communist prisons because his faith in Christ. He was often tortured, and on some occasions nearly starved to death. But the principle of tithing was so internalized in his heart that when he was given one slice of bread a week and dirty soup every day, he faithfully tithed from it. Every tenth day he gave his soup to a weaker brother, and every tenth week he took his slice of bread and gave it to one of his fellow prisoners in Jesus' name.

Henry Crowell, founder of the Quaker Oats Company and a significant contributor to the work of Moody Bible Institute knew how to use money wisely. As a young man, he received Christ as his Savior. When he began his business career in a little Ohio factor, he promised God that he would honor Him in his giving. God's blessing was upon him; and, as his business grew, he increased his giving. After more than forty years of giving 60 percent of his income to God, Crowell testified, "I've never gotten ahead of God. He has always been ahead of me in giving."

The only investments I ever made which have paid constantly increasing dividends is the money I have given to the Lord said J. L. Kraft, head of Kraft Cheese, who for many years gave 25% of his income to Christian causes

I have tithed every dollar God has entrusted to me: And I want to say, if I had not tithed the first dollar I made, I would not have tithed the first million dollars I made said John D. Rockefeller, Sr.

I am totally dependent on God for help in everything I do. Otherwise I honestly believe I would start to fall apart in months said Wallace Johnson, founder of Holiday Inn and a Christian

GOD'S PLAN OF PEOPLE MANAGEMENT

ALONE: The Adversary of Leadership.

In the book of Numbers we have a record of probably the largest business meeting that was ever convened. Twelve men had been selected to view the land God had given His chosen that He had delivered from Egypt. After viewing the cities for their strength, the land for its productiveness, and the people as for quantity. They returned with their report. Ten saw giants in the land. Only two saw what they could do. Caleb's record is in Numbers 13:30, "Let us go up at once and possess it for we are able to overtake it."

I. THE CHALLENGE OF - - - - - - - - - - "LET US."

Proverbs 6: 16-19 describes seven things "which are an abomination" to GOD. "Haughty eyes, a lying tongue, and hands that shed innocent blood, a heart that devises wicked plans, feet that make haste to run to evil, a false witness who breathes out lies, and a man who sows discord among brothers." All of these seven things God hate cause bad relationships between people. Six of the Ten Commandments deal directly with man's relationship with his fellow man.

Studies conducted by *Management Training Systems* indicate that 90% of all job turnovers is connected with relationship problems. Therefore, maintaining good relationships is important to organizational stability and productivity. This percentage can be said of the average church as well.

WHAT YOU SHOULD KNOW ABOUT RELATIONSHIPS

- All relationships revolve around personal needs.
- Contact alters relationships.
- Relationships are constantly changing.
- Met needs build relationships.
- Unmet needs erode relationships.

THE FOUR RELATIONSHIP STYLES

There are four basic relationship styles: Cooperation. Retaliation, Domination and Isolation. All relationships begin in a Cooperation style and remain there as long as all needs within the relationship are being met.

An unmet need causes the person with the need to move to a Retaliation style of relationship in an effort to get his or her need met. This relationship style focuses on a struggle to get the other person to meet the unmet need.

Eventually there is what appear to be a winner and a loser. At this point a new relationship begins called Domination. During this period of the relationship the person losing the struggle for control is dominated by the person "winning" the struggle.

After a period of time the person being dominated concludes he is being rejected and the situation is hopeless. At this point he takes the first step to a new relationship style--Isolation. An Isolation relationship style is the last phase of a deteriorating relationship before termination.

Leaders and members are in one of these four relationship styles with people at all times. The farther one moves away from a Cooperation style the lower productivity drops. The greatest level of satisfaction is maintained within the Cooperation style. Therefore, the leader must focus on maintaining an atmosphere of cooperation within his team or work group and membership.

CONDITIONS WITHIN THE COOPERATION STYLE

Psalms 133:1 says. "Behold, how good and how pleasant it is for brethren to dwell together in unity!" As long as people maintain a cooperation style relationship the following conditions will exist within the team:

- There will be a commitment to meet the other person's needs.
- Mutual trust and respect will exist.
- There will be mutual utilization of personal skills and creativity.
- Problems will be solved jointly.
- Productivity will increase.
- Commitment to the relationship will grow.

This is the type of relationship Jesus described in Matthew 7:12 when he said, 'Therefore, whatever you want men to do to you, do also to them, for this is the Law and the Prophets."

CONDITIONS WITHIN THE RETALIATION STYLE

In Matthew 5:38-42 Jesus criticized people who retaliate by saying. "The Law of Moses says. 'If a man gouges out another's eye, he must pay with his own eye. If a tooth gets knocked out, knock out the tooth of the one who did it.' But I say: Don't, resist violence! If you are slapped on one cheek, turn the other too. If you are ordered to court, and your shirt is taken from you, give your coat too. If the military demands that you carry their gear for a mile, carry it two. Give to those who ask, and don't turn away from those who want to borrow." (Paraphrase)

The Retaliation style contains the following conditions:

- There are attempts to make the other person conform to what you want done.
- Aggressive action toward the other person is eventually taken.
- The other person becomes an object in your way, not a person with his own needs.
- A struggle for domination begins.
- There is a period of perpetual conflict.
- Eventually there appears to be a winner and loser.

CONDITIONS WITHIN THE DOMINATION STYLE

The Domination style contains the following conditions:

- The "loser's controlled by the "winner."
- The loser's personality is "suffocated."
- Each loses respect for the other.
- The loser's creativity is lost.
- The loser resorts to manipulation.
- The loser gives up--concludes the situation is hopeless--and the relationship will not improve.

CONDITIONS WITHIN ISOLATION STYLE

The following conditions exist within the Isolation style:

- The other person is mentally blocked out.

- Communication stops.
- Both develop mistrust of the other.
- Problems remain unsolved.
- Needs remain unmet.
- Each develops unconcern for the other's needs.
- Productivity within the relationship drops drastically.
- Relationship terminates.

RESTORING RELATIONSHIPS TO COOPERATION

The key to maintaining good relationships is to know what to do when the relationship starts to deteriorate. Many Christians have allowed themselves to be deceived into believing a godly person never has problems in relationships. Such thinking is very dangerous because it leads one to assume that if he has relationship problems, it is a sign he is not very mature in his relationship with Christ. Therefore, the tendency is for the Christian to suppress the problem and not bring it out into the open so it can be dealt with and solved. One should keep in mind that it is the suppression of--and failure to deal with--relationship problems that indicate spiritual immaturity, and not necessarily the problem itself.

No one is immune from relationship problems. The mature person faces them when they occur, and commits himself to finding a solution. On the other hand, the immature person frequently tries to ignore the problem and avoids dealing with the issues involved. Such action is not Scriptural.

Jesus said, "So if you are standing before the altar in the temple, offering a sacrifice to GOD, and suddenly remember that a. friend has something against you, leave your sacrifice there beside the altar and go and apologize and be reconciled to him. and then come and offer your sacrifice to GOD." Matthew 5:23-24 (Paraphrased)

As soon as a relationship moves out of the Cooperation style the following steps should be taken:

Admit your current relationship style (James 5: 16) Admit your selfishness is sin and ask God and the others involved to forgive you. (Colossians 3: 13 and Matthew 6:14-15).

Make a decision to develop a cooperation style relationship (Philippians 2:34).

Begin acting out I Corinthians 13:4-8.

Start thanking God for those in the relationship (I Thessalonians 5: 18).

The steps listed above are not necessarily easy: however, God has given these principles as a means of restoring relationships to a cooperative and productive state.

RULES FOR RIGHT RELATIONSHIPS

In order to maintain a Cooperation style relationship apply the following rules:

1. Attack the problem...not the person. If you attack the person instead of the problem you will cause the relationship to move out of cooperation into retaliation.
2. Verbalize feelings...don't act them out. State how you feel and why, instead of communicating your feelings by the way you act.
3. Forgive in place of judging. When you are wronged forgive the person involved. Don't judge the person for his actions.

4. Be committed to give more than you take. The key to a cooperation relationship is giving more than you take. Always focus on meeting the needs of the other person. If everyone in the relationship does this all needs will continually be met.

II. THE CHALLENGE OF - - - - - - - - - - GO"

A. Suggests an Outward look.

"Go into all the world" ...Matt. 28:19

B. General Douglas MacArthur motto:

You are as young as your faith
as old as your doubt.
As young as your confidence
as old as your fear.
As young as your hope
as old as your despair.

C. "It is your Fathers good pleasure to give you the Kingdom" - Luke 12:32

D. "I know thy works, that thou art neither cold nor hot: I would thou wert cold or hot. so then because thou art lukewarm. and neither cold nor hot. I will spew thee out of my mouth." -Rev. 3:15- 16.

III. THE CHALLENGE OF - - - - - - - - - - - "UP"

A. "I am with you always" -Matt. 28:20

B. "If God be for us, who can be against us" -Romans 8:3.

C. "God shall help. And that right early" -Psalm 46:5.

D. "God is our refuge and strength, a very present help in trouble" -Psalm 46: 1.

E. The long road of Theodore Sauder.

F. Songs of C.A. Tingley,. Jr.

IV. THE CHALLENGE OF - - - - - - - - - - - - "AT ONCE."

A. "Today if you hear my voice harden not your hearts as in the days provocation." -Heb. 3:8.

B. "Today is the day of salvation."

C. The apostles counted it an honor "that they were found worthy to be persecuted for Christ."

D. There is little compassion today.

V. THE CHALLENGE OF - - - - - - - - "AND POSSESS IT."

A. D. L. Moody preached to more than 100 million with 1 million coming to Christ. The results of his labor still remain.

B. Pastor Ki of Korea.

C. S.M. Park of Brazil.

VI. THE CHALLENGE OF - - - - - - - - - "FOR WE ARE ABLE."

While Caleb and Joshua were alone and without any support for their follower, they did what was right and remained true to the convictions they held. Joshua 14:7-15 records the wish and the events that followed of Caleb's 85th birthday. "Give me that mountain" is still a common cry of those whose faith continues.

Loneliness is perhaps the strongest foe many of us will ever face. It creates the sensation of being cut off, of being isolated from those who are closest and most important to you, and of having no meaningful relationship with anyone who truly cares. People often feel lonely even with family and friends nearby.

There is a difference between loneliness and aloneness. Being alone can be depressing, but it can also be used by god to minister to your spirit and feelings in an intimate way. Aloneness can be good and beneficial, while loneliness is hard for any of us to take.

Only you can control the extent of your loneliness. You can choose to remain melancholy and depressed, or you can focus on brighter. More positive realities (Phil. 4:8, 3:12-15). If you are a Christian, realize you are not cut off--you have the holy spirit within you (Eph. 3:16). Additionally, the lord himself promises never to leave you or forsake you (Heb. 13:5, matt. 28:20). Earthly relationships are obviously important, but you don't have to depend on them for your mental well-being. The Christian can be absolutely alone without being lonely or depressed. It all comes down to how you choose to handle your salvation.

Delight in god's word (ps. 119:14, 16, 24, 50), pursue worthwhile activities that contribute to someone else's benefit, and discipline yourself to meditate often upon great spiritual truths. Practice personal worship in such a way that solitude is a friend, not an enemy. Finally, Consider the people around you to be your personal ministry. Give yourself completely to serving them (Phil. 2:3-4). If you do, your loneliness will be replaced with satisfaction and genuine contentment.

II. BEHAVIOR: The Basis of Proper Relationships

A. HUMAN BEHAVIOR IS MANAGEABLE

I. Requirements for those who lead

A). Authority by which a leader manages

1). The authority of competence
2). The authority of position
3). The authority of your personality
4). The authority of character

B). Steps in effective leading and direction

1). Communication
2). Faith and confidence in one's own ability
3). Faith and confidence in other people
4). Knowledge of human nature and behavior
5). Proper delegation
6). Trestle and bridge-building.
(public relations)

C). What a leader must prepare in advance

1). Establish a system for evaluating personnel, workers or followers
2). Establish a system of checks and controls
3). Establish a system of motivation & rewards
4). Establish a system of discipline
5). Ensure that the ideas, people, things, time and other elements of leadership will be available at the right time, in the right place, in the right quantities

2. RELATIONSHIP WITH THOSE WHO ARE LED

a).

I. Appreciate people for who they
II. Are anticipate they will do their best
III. Admire their accomplishments
IV. Accept your personal responsibility

I'm just a plow hand from Arkansas, but I have learned how to hold a team together--how to lift some men up, how to calm down others, until finally they've got one heartbeat together, a team. There's just three things I'd ever say: If anything goes bad, I did it. If anything goes semi-good, then we did it. If anything goes really well, then you did it. That's all it takes to get people to win football games for you.

--Bear Bryant

---

b). SIX BASIC TYPES OF PROBLEMS

1). Problems with ideas
2). Problems with people
3). Problems with things
4). Problems with time
5). Problems with leadership
6). Problems with faith

c). LEADERSHIP MAY BE USED IN THREE WAYS

1). Doing things "to" the people (Exodus 18:14)
2). Doing things "for" the people
3). Doing things "through" he people (Exodus 18:21-22)

3. RESISTANCE FROM THOSE WHO LABOR

If you could change one thing about your church. what would it be? Would it be a change in facilities, scheduling, curriculum, organization, personnel, equipment, or training? If you made all these changes at once what would be the results or reactions?

a). WHY PEOPLE RESIST CHANGE

1). Loss of security. The unknown, the unfamiliar are frightening and unpredictable. The new and different are strange and uncomfortable. The familiar is preferred. People like to know what to expect. Change may result in loss of security.

2). Threatened personal status or position. An Individual's vested interest may appear to be at stake. Even something as simple as changing from one classroom to another may cause resistance.

3). Implied criticism of the present. New ideas suggest dissatisfaction with the way things are done now. It may suggest that the old way is not good enough, (which it may not be). Yet many people are satisfied with the status quo.

4). Seems unnecessary or unhelpful. For some the present situation is satisfactory. For others it's utterly hopeless. Or an idea may be resisted because something similar was tried before without success.

Two words that can kill any new ideas are never and always, as in "We never did it that way before," or "'We always did it this way."

b). PREVENTING RESISTANCE TO CHANGE

In spite of your best efforts, resistance to change will probably exist. How can you handle it. There are these possibilities.

First, you can feel that the opposition is a personal threat and resign from your position with hurt feelings.

Second, you can forcibly impose the change. In spite of resistance and lose your co-workers' confidence and cooperation. If you follow this approach, begin looking for a new staff of workers.

Third, remember all resistance is not bad. It may force you to reevaluate the proposed change. You may change it, strengthen and improve it.

Fourth, Express understanding for an opposite viewpoint. Try to see the situation from the other person's vantage point.

Fifth, Admit strength in others' positions. Realize that no idea is all good or all bad. If you admit the good points, the opposition may admit yours.

Sixth, Evaluate objections with the individual. Think through each argument point-for-point. It may reveal the weaknesses of the objection.

Seventh, When opposition is intense. Shift into neutral. Don't try to win every issue. You may win a point and lose the respect and services of an otherwise good worker. Anything worthwhile is worth waiting for.

c). PRESENTING NEW IDEAS AND CHANGES

What can you do to help people feel the need for change and accept it more readily?

1). Carefully present there exists a sense of dissatisfaction with the status quo. Periodically evaluate programs and structures. Let the facts speak for themselves. Use your records to point out a need for change. Chart attendance for the year. Compare it with the previous year. Let the facts speak.

2). Let people share in planning for change. People will more likely accept change if they think the new idea is theirs and they're involved in the planning.

3). Give forewarning of any proposed change. Don't spring new ideas and changes on people. Keep them informed as the change takes place.

4). Begin by making small changes. Sweeping revisions can start with a simple step In the right direction

d). PRINCIPLES FOR PRESENTING A NEW IDEA

1). Don't oversell it. Avoid high-pressure tactics.

2). Watch your timing. Be aware of extenuating circumstances that might affect the outcome. Take note of' the group atmosphere and attitudes.

3). Be positive. Stress the advantages. List the pros and cons and try to answer objections in your presentation.

4). Give people a chance to think it over and talk about it. Give them a chance to get used to the new idea.

5). Pray about each new idea. Rely on the Holy Spirit to break down barriers. Open closed minds. Dissolve resistance and create a readiness to change.

As a leader who encourages people to accept and adjust to change be personable. Be human. Exhibit a spirit of humility. Win and hold their respect. Express personal interest in others as individuals. Keep a sense of humor. Don't take yourself too seriously.

You can change things and live to talk about it!

THE TEN COMMANDMENTS OF HUMAN RELATIONS

1. SPEAK TO PEOPLE. There is nothing as nice as a cheerful word.
2. SMILE AT PEOPLE. It takes 72 muscles to frown and only 14 to smile.
3. CALL PEOPLE BY NAME. The sweetest music to many ears is the sound of one's own name.
4. BE FRIENDLY AND HELPFUL. If you would have friends, be friendly.
5. BE CORDIAL. Speak and act as though everything you do is a genuine pleasure.
6. HAVE A GENUINE INTEREST IN PEOPLE.
7. BE GENEROUS WITH PRAISE. CAUTIOUS WITH CRITICISM.
8. BE CONSIDERATE OF THE FEELINGS OF OTHERS. There are three sides to a controversy: yours, the other side, and the right one.
9. BE THOUGHTFUL OF THE OPINIONS OF OTHERS.
10. BE ALERT TO GIVE SERVICE. What counts most in life is what we do for others.

B. HUMAN BEHAVIOR CAN BE MOTIVATED

1. UNDERSTANDING MOTIVATION

A). Motivation is psychological, not logical
B). Motivation is fundamentally an unconscious process
C). Motivation is an individual matter

D). Motivating needs differ from person to person
E). Motivation is inevitably a social process

2. MOTIVATION IS PERSON RELATED

A). Behavior depends on both the person and his environment
B). Each individual behaves in ways, which make sense to him
C). An individual's perception of a situation influences his behavior in that situation
D). An individual's view of himself influences what he does
E). An individual's behavior is influenced by his needs
F). Everyone is motivated at some level
G). Motivation always involves some goal
H). Motivations are learned not inherited
I). Human desires precedes motivation
J). Motivation is more effective when a man has a clear concept of his goal
K). Motivation is inseparable from one's values, needs, and desires
L). Motivation begins where the person is
M). Information regarding a goals distance is motivation
N) the "terms" of one's motivation are "defined" by the individual
O). One's self image is related to the direction and limits of his motivation

3. HOW TO MOTIVATE

A). Communicate standards (be consistent)
B). Be aware Of your own biases and prejudices
C.) Let people know where they stand
D.) Give praise when it is appropriate

E.) Keep people informed of changes that may affect them
F.) Care about your people
G.) Perceive people as ends, not means
H.) Go out of your way to help people
I.) Take responsibility for your people
J.) Build independence
K.) Exhibit personal diligence

4. HOW NOT MOTIVATE

A). Never belittle a subordinate
(Destroys self-worth)
B). Never criticize a subordinate in front of others
(Destroys rapport)
C). Give subordinates your undivided attention
(self-respect disappears)
D). Never seem preoccupied with your own interests
(Gives impression of selfishness and manipulation of others for your own purposes)
E). Never play favorites
(destroys morale)
F). Never fail to help your sub-ordinates grow
G). Never be insensitive to small things
H). Never embarrass weak followers
I). Never vacillate in making a decision

5. WHAT MOTIVATES PEOPLE

A). Achievement
B). Recognition
C). Work itself
D). Responsibility
E). Advancement

F). Competence/fairness of leader
G). Interpersonal relationship
H). Working conditions

C. HUMAN BEHAVIOR IS OFTEN MISUNDERSTOOD

I. REALITIES ABOUT MISUNDERSTANDING

A). Misunderstanding is rarely the fault of any one person
B). Misunderstanding is seldom voluntary
C). Misunderstanding is always pre- ceded by some cause
D). Misunderstanding usually affects, both parties
E). Misunderstanding, regardless of severity, need not mean the termination of what was previously a wholesome relationship

2. REASONS FOR MISUNDERSTANDING

A). Our experiences are different
B). Our perceptions of ourselves are different
C). Our images of others are different
D). Our needs and wants are different
E). Our values are different
F). Our problems are different
G). Our secrets are different
H). Our definitions are different
I). Our abilities to communicate are different
J). Our perceptions of expectations from others are different
K). What we see is different

L). We think others are like us
M). Misinterpretations of intermediaries cause misunderstanding

III. COMMUNICATION: The Craft of Create Fellowship

What is communication? Most people admit they have communication problems from time to time, but few people clearly understand what communication is. Communication can be defined as: the process we go through to convey understanding from one person or group to another. Unless understanding occurs we have not communicated.

In Genesis 11:7 God said, "Come, let us you down and there confuse their language. that they may not understand one another's speech." (NKJV). God knew good communication is the key to organizational success. Since the people's goal was not the will of God he stopped work on the project by disrupting their communication system. The passage goes on to explain in verse 8 that when their communication system broke down. It destroyed their unity and commitment to work and the people were scattered. Therefore, communication is the life blood of the organization. That is, it is the key to unity and commitment.

Jesus knew the importance of communication and he worked with his disciples to make sure understanding took place. After sharing several parables with them in Matthew 13:36-50, Jesus asked, "Have you understood all these things?" Matthew 13:51 (NKJV). He wanted to make sure he was communicating.

UNDERSTANDING THE COMMUNICATION PROCESS

Step One: Develop a clear concept of the idea or feeling to be communicated. All communication focuses around the transmitting of ideas and/or feelings. If a person doesn't know what he is trying to say, the people receiving the message will not understand what he is saying.

Step Two: Choose the right words and actions to convey the idea and/or feeling. Ideas and feelings are transmitted through words and actions. Therefore, it is important to make sure right words and actions are used in transmitting the desired message. The wrong action or word can distort the message, causing misunderstanding.

Step Three: (The barriers to communication). A series of barriers stand in the way between sending a message and receiving what was said. These barriers may vary slightly from organization to organization and person to person. It is important to identify and eliminate them in order to develop and maintain effective communication.

Step Four: The listener receives the information. The listener or receiver of the information plays a very important role in the development of understanding. His first job is to listen to the ideas and feelings being transmitted to him. Therefore, listening plays a very important role in the process of developing understanding. More will be said about this later.

Step Five: The receiver translates words and actions into ideas and feelings: The translation of words and actions into ideas and feelings is a very critical step in the development of understanding. A great deal of the idea and feeling can be lost during this phase of the process.

Step Six: The receiver develops an idea and feeling. If the idea and feeling being sent in step one is the same idea and feeling being received in step six, understanding occurs and those involved have communicated effectively. On the other hand, if the idea and feeling in step six is different than the idea and feeling sent in step one, we have misunderstanding and no communication. Therefore, the goal is to make sure the idea and feeling sent is the idea and feeling received. This Is accomplished by feeding back the ideas and feelings heard.

THE IMPORTANCE OF DISCLOSURE AND FEEDBACK

Honesty in the form of being willing to disclose true ideas and feelings plays an important part in the development of understanding between individuals and groups. The person unwilling to disclose his ideas and feelings cannot experience effective communication. Honest disclosure makes known to others what is known to you. On the other hand, feedback from others allows you to know what others know. Without disclosure and feedback people cannot experience good communication.

Jesus worked on developing understanding between himself and his disciples by the use of disclosure and feedback. As he taught them who he was he sought feedback to make sure they understood. This is demonstrated in Matthew 16:13-16, "...he asked his disciples, who do men say that I, the Son of man am? So they said, some say John the Baptist, some Elijah. and others Jeremiah or one of the prophets, He said to them, but who do you say that I am? Simon Peter answered and said, you are the Christ, the Son of the Living God." (NKJV}

In this discussion Jesus asked for feedback from the disciples concerning their thoughts about him in order to determine their level of understanding. This is an important and necessary tool of communication.

THE ROLE OF NON-VERBAL COMMUNICATION

Studies have shown that most ideas and feelings are transmitted non-verbally. This means what you "do" communicates far more than what you "say". Most messages are communicated in the following way:

- 55% of the message is communicated non-verbally.
- 38% is communicated through tone of voice.
- 7% is communicated by actual words.

This means that 93% of all ideas and feelings are communicated through some form of non-verbal means--either actions or the way we say a word. Therefore, how you say a word becomes more important than the word itself. This also indicates that most of the misunderstanding is communication occurs within the non-verbal area of communication.

THE IMPORTANCE OF PERCEPTIVE LISTENING

Since 93% of the message is communicated non-verbally. It becomes extremely important for the listener to make sure he translates the message properly. For example, in Mark 8:11-21 It is obvious the disciples had misunderstood Jesus. Part of it was due to improper listening. Therefore, listening skills play a very important role in the development of understanding.

PASSIVE LISTENING VS. PERCEPTIVE LISTENING

The person using "passive" listening is only hearing the words being spoken. Therefore, he receives approximately 7% of the true ideas and feelings being transmitted. In the example In Mark 8: 11-21 the disciples were using passive listening. They heard only the words Christ spoke and missed the meaning behind the words. Passive listening always fails to hear the meaning. Ideas and feelings behind the words being spoken.

On the other hand, perceptive listening focuses on the actions and tone of voice as well as the meaning, attitudes and feelings behind the words being spoken. The person using perceptive listening hears far more than just the words being spoken. He also hears the other 93% of the message that is being transmitted non-verbally. It has been said. "words do not have meaning. people have meaning for words." That is why every person needs to learn to use perceptive listening skill. Perceptive listening allows the person to hear the real meaning attached to the words being used to communicate ideas and feelings.

ATTITUDES NEEDED WHEN USING PERCEPTIVE LISTENING

The person using perceptive listening techniques must want to hear the real feelings and attitudes of the person sending the message. He must also be willing to accept the attitudes and feelings being communicated. And finally, he must have a desire to assist in any way possible.

The person unwilling to accept the real feelings of others and help where needed is wasting his or her time using perceptive listening skills.

A. DEVELOPING C H A R I S M A

1. CHARISMA

c-oncern -the ability to show you care
h-elp -the ability to reach out
a-ction -the ability to make things happen
r-esults -the ability to produce
i-nfluence -the ability to lead
s-ensitivity -the ability to feel/respond

m-otivation - the ability to give hope
a-ffirmation -the ability to build up

Be more concerned about making others feel good about themselves than you are in making them feel good about you.

Ask yourself what draws you to people? Try to understand and develop the qualities you enjoy in others

2. FIVE WAYS YOU WANT OTHERS TO TREAT YOU

A). You want others to encourage you
B). You want others to appreciate you
C). You want others to forgive you
D). You want others to listen to you
E). You want others to understand you

3. DO YOU KNOW WHAT DRAWS PEOPLE TO YOU? EVALUATE WHAT PEOPLE LIKE ABOUT YOU AND WHY

B. DEALING WITH CRITICISM

I. HOW TO GIVE CRITICISM

A). Check your motive
B). Make sure the issue is worthy of criticism
C). Be specific
D). Don't undermine the person's self- confidence
E). Don't compare one person with another
F). Be creative or don't confront
G). Attack the problem not the person
H). Wait until the time is right
I). Look at yourself before looking at others
J). End meeting with encouragement

Leaders have a story of not being able to take criticism. No one has the right to give it if they are unable to receive it in return.

Each of us learn from others and it can be a valuable teaching experience. Become a person who can handle criticism learn to use to use this type confrontation as an opportunity to grow.

TO TAKE CRITICISM

A). Understand the difference between constructive and destructive criticism
B). Don't take yourself too seriously
C). Look beyond the criticism and see the critic
D). Watch your attitude toward the critic
E). Realize that good people get criticized
F). Keep physically and spiritually in shape
G). Don't just see the critic: see if there's a crowd
H). Wait for time to prove them wrong
I). Surround yourself with positive people
J). Concentrate on your mission
--change your mistakes

My close friend, Dr. Charles Thigpen, former President of Welch College, shared the following with me when I was in the position of being criticized:

- Listen to it
- Learn from it
- Love through it
- Live above it!

God's Word has much to say to the Christian leader, pastor, manager, supervisor, or boss.

The apostle Paul wrote. "Masters, grant to your slaves justice and fairness, knowing that you too have a Master in heaven" (Col. 4: 1). The Greek word translated "justice" (dikaios) is the biblical word for righteousness. It means to be just in the sense of judging without prejudice or partiality. It also indicates a state of being right or right conduct, whether judged by divine or human standards.

The word translated “fairness” in Colossians 4:1 is translated "equally" in 2 Corinthians 8: 14. It conveys not equality of condition but brotherly equality growing out of the Christian relation, in which there is neither slave nor free.

Ephesians 6:9 adds, "Masters, do the same things to them, and give up threatening, knowing that both their master and yours is in heaven, and there is no partially with Him.” In context the apostle was saying that a master should treat his servants with the same attitudes with which his servants are to treat him, namely respect, sincerity, and good will.

No matter how high you are in any system, whether president, chairman of the board, pastor, or church secretary, remember that you have a Master in heaven. Treat peers or followers as you would like to be treated if you were in their place.

"Give up threatening" implies that threatening was a common weapon masters used against their slaves. Threatening is not only a bad witness for a Christian boss, leader, or etc., but also a poor management technique. Motivate your employees with positive reinforcement, and be sure to pay them fairly. As Scripture teaches, “The laborer is worthy of his wages” (Luke 10:7; I Tim. 5: 18). That is much more effective in building mutual trust and respect between an employer and employee than threats and bullying.

If you are a leader, supervisor or boss, God has placed you in a position of authority. Never use that position to crush the spirit of one who is serving you.

Supervision or management is being done with "no partiality." The Greek word translated "partiality" refers to favoritism. Those in charge are not to show preference for the position, rank, popularity, or earthly circumstances of any man or woman. To favor the rich, famous, or powerful over the common or ordinary man is to ignore the real value of the inner man.

The New Testament standard reminds those over others, that although by God's grace he has been given authority on earth over his followers he too is under authority: that of his heavenly Master. Please your Master by treating your followers fairly and compassionately.

PLUG INTO THE CHURCH FOR THE SHOCK OF YOUR LIFE

INTRODUCTION: A number of years ago I preached on the Church in Dayton, Ohio when afterwards fourteen year old girl told me "I really enjoyed your sermon this morning but the title was too bland." I thanked her for her compliment and ask what she would have changed it to. She said a sermon should have something electric in it. I would have called your sermon today, *"Plug into the Church for the Shock of your Life!"* From then on I have used her title and will do so today since I want to preach to you about the church.

Years ago when I was in college I heard the noted Quaker preacher, Dr. Elton Trueblood, preach on the *Bigness of the Church.* I remember well his remarks. He said "To many the church is when you are driving down a street and see a sign that says Church zone and you look at a building made of stone or timber and continue until you come to the end of the church zone and think that is the church." His conclusion was we are the church as we are at our job, or at school, or at the bank. This is when the church is at its best....or its worst.

My dear friend and Dayton pastor, Dr. Hobart Ashby said, *"There are no small churches-The church is a big business. It is the only business that reaches from time to eternity."*

I enjoy church signs and record them as I drive down the highway. Recently, I read one on a Methodist church I liked. It said, "Join us today for a faith lift!" One of my favorites was on the sign of a Mennonite church in Ohio. “All sinners not welcome.” Which disturbed me until I read the next line, “For we only have room for 350.” One I read in Alabama said, “When you were born you cried and the world rejoiced. When you died you rejoiced and the world cried.” Lastly church sign in Tennessee stated, “Sorrow looks back, worry looks around, faith looks up.”

Raymond C. Ortlund in his book, *LET THE CHURCH BE THE CHURCH,* tells of a pilot who announced over his intercom system, "Ladies and gentlemen, I have good news and bad news. The good news in that we have a tailwind and are making excellent time. The bad news is that our compass is broken and we have no idea where we are going."

There is a story in *THE LAST HURRAH* that illustrates my concern. The mayor of Boston is watching a parade. He says, *"There go the people. I am their leader. I must follow them."*

I. CONGREGATE

For many years I have reviewed the church in the Bible. The word Church appears 77 times, Assembly 49, sanctuary 137, but congregate 364 places in both testaments.

In Psalm 78:54 a beautiful thought appears, *"And He brought them to the border of His Sanctuary...which His right hand purchased."*

We congregate for a number of reasons but let me look at two:

1. We congregate because we are a part of a **permanent union**. *"There is neither Jew nor Greek, there is neither slave or free, there is neither male nor female; for you are all one in Christ Jesus."* Gal.3:28.

2. We congregate **because Jesus Christ is alive and coming again."** *Not forsaking the assembling of ourselves together, as the manner of some, but exhorting one another, and so much the more as you see the day approaching."* Heb. 10:25.

Illustration: Years ago there were two churches in Kentucky that were jointly praying weekly for a brewery in their town to close down some way. After an evening of praying the people returned home and a storm came and lighting struck the distillery and burn the entire building down. Do I have to tell what these two churches preached about that morning? The owner of this business was an Atheist and he heard about the churches boasting of their responsibly for the destruction. The businessman sued the two churches and before the judge attempted to disprove what they had spread as truth. After much deliberation the judge made a damaging statement. "As I have listened to all in this preceding, it appears to me we have two churches that down deny the strength of their prayers, and now I see an atheist who now believes in the power of prayer."

Do were like them deny the power of prayer? Has our vision stopped?

YOU WILL KNOW THAT YOU HAVE A GOD-SIZE VISION WHEN IT MEETS THE FOLLOWING CRITERIA:

a. It originates with God.
b. It is centered in and supported by His Word.
c. It requires supernatural empowering.
d. It is grounded in the Great Commission.
e. It leads the church to exalt Christ.
f. It requires radical obedience.
g. It produces natural growth.
h. It demands a willingness to change.
i. It requires every church member's best effort.

II. CELEBRATE

The church is a place where we should celebrate because we have victory and able to give praise and honor to Him.

"Oh come, let us sing to the Lord! Let us shout joyfully to the rock of our salvation. Let us come before His presence with thanksgiving; let us shout to him with Psalms" Ps.95:1

"It shall be a Sabbath of rest...from even unto even, ye shall celebrate your Sabbath." Lev. 23:32

Illustration: I was invited to Annapolis to marry young man who would graduate from the naval academy and to a young lady from our church in Columbus, Ohio. We arrive early for the commencement and it didn't last long for the stadium to fill to its capacity with thousands of people. I began to watch as the dignitaries found their place on the stage observing the dress uniforms of many high ranking navy and marine officers and the colorful robes of the academia. I was in awe with the pageantry of the affair.

Then I watched as 1014 young men and women marched to their seats in the middle of the field which awaited them. In a short time each would be awarded a commission in either the Navy or Marines --an event they had waited for four years.

After they were seated, and the designated speakers had all finished, the president of the academy acknowledged the person who graduated first in the class. The crowd replied with a thundering applause. As each student was recognized and came across the platform, I noticed that President Bush greeted each one after the award.

By now it is about 11:30 a.m. and my body was back in slumberville. I would not stay there long as I was awaken by an applause that was even greater than that given the very first fellow. I turned to the young lady who I would marry to a newly commissioned marine within hours, and asked what the sudden stir all about was. Her answer caused a query when she said, *"Oh, he is the one who is graduating last in the class."* Last in the class? I muttered. Then she said, *"There is an old naval academy custom that the one who graduates last receive a standing ovation because he saves the other grads from the humiliation of being last."* She continued by telling me that all the others will give him one dollar for the same reason. Well, my math teacher would have been proud when I immediately shouted $1013 dollars?

By now he was on the platform receiving his award. He jumped with excitement and stopping just long enough as he shook the hand of the nation's president. At which time President Bush, a former naval graduate himself, who probably knew this custom, slipped off his watch and gives it to him. I thought to myself, I bet it wasn't a Timex!

As he departed this happy guy was holding high his certificate with both hands jumping all over the platform oblivious of all the important men and women all around him.

As I observed this excited lad back to his seat, I was reminded that the academic Dean in his address revealed that 167 students that started with this class had failed to finish with them. No wonder he was rejoicing. He may have finished last-but he finished.

Let us consider the many that used to be regular in church that have dropped from their attendance. Will they graduate?

We celebrate by singing, giving thanks, sharing our offering, encouraging one another, reading and hearing God's word and reaching to others to celebrate with us in Christ.

Church specialists tell us why churches fail. Let's do a check to find where our church may be:

1: Loss of evangelistic focus
2: Loss of emphasis and commitment
3: Loss of vision for the total work of the Sunday school
4: Dismantling the component parts
5: Lack of a clear purpose statement
6: Fear of innovation

III. COMMEMORATE

We should remember especially the following things.

1. AT THE TABLE as we remember His death, resurrection and coming again

2. IN OUR TESTIMONY as we commemorates His birth, baptism, death, resurrection, coming of the Holy Spirit.

Don't ever forget that although you may succeed beyond your fondest hopes and your greatest expectations, you will never succeed beyond the purpose to which you are willing to surrender. *"Seek first the kingdom of God and His righteousness and all of these other things shall be added unto you."* Matt. 6:33.

The secret of the surrendered life is giving God

The first part of every day,
The first day of every week,

The first portion of you income,
The first consideration in every decision, and
The first place in all of your life.

When we surrender to Him, then we have a power that really caps off the formula for success. Surrender is what brings power.

We fight for power and we lose it;
we surrender and we find it.

IV. COMMUNICATE

The church has many purposes but I want to stress these.

1. PREACHING

Notice the following recipe for revival is made up of:

People that are dedicated
Preaching that disturbs
Prayer that is definite
Power that is divine

4. **PROCLAMATION**: Worships involves witness to God, church, and lost world.

Today the purposes are unchanged
The church exists to:
Edify
Encourage
Exalt
Equip
Evangelize

Deuteronomy 6:4-9:

Hear, O Israel: The Lord our God is one Lord:

And thou shalt love the Lord thy God with all thine heart, and with all thy soul, and with all thy might.

And these words, which I command thee this day, shall be in thine heart:

And thou shalt teach them diligently unto thy children, and shalt talk of them when thou sittest in thine house, and when thou walkest by the way, and when thou liest down, and when thou risest up.

And thou shalt bind them for a sign upon thine hand, and they shall be as frontlets between thine eyes.

And thou shalt write them upon the posts of thy house, and on thy gates.

This passage is central to Jewish life and worship. The Jews call it the Shema, which is the Jewish word for "Hear", as in, "Hear, O Israel." The Jews quote this verse in all their services, and every Jew is to recite it every morning and every evening. It is also the traditional words recited at the time of death or of martyrdom. To the Jews, this one passage, more than any other Old Testament Scripture, sums up their beliefs and their duties.

According to the Gospel of Mark, Jesus quoted from the Shema during a dispute with the scribes (Mark 12:28-30). "And one of the scribes came, and having heard them reasoning together, and perceiving that he had answered them well, asked him, which is the first commandment of all? And Jesus answered him, the first of all the commandments is, Hear, O Israel; The Lord our God is one Lord: And thou shalt love the Lord thy God with all thy heart, and with all thy soul, and with all thy mind, and with all thy strength: this is the first commandment."

It says three things to me about Christian parenting. We must carefully perform three duties if we want to instill Jesus Christ into the hearts of our children.

I love the writing of Robert Morgan concerning this material. Note his words below as a responsibility for us.

1. **Love Your God Deeply**

First, we are to love the Lord our God with all our heart and with all our strength.

A. There are two principles here. The first is one of **derivation.** We derive from God the love, wisdom, and strength that we need in child-rearing. You cannot adequately love your child until you deeply love your God.

The Bible says, *"Dear friends, let us love one another, for love comes from God. Everyone who loves has been born of God and knows God."*

B. There's a second reason for loving God first. Not only derivation, but **demonstration.**

Children learn best by modeling. If they see in you a genuine, warm love for Christ, they will desire the same.

Do you remember the story of the little boy in Sunday school? The teacher asked him why he loved God, and, after thinking a moment, he said, *"I guess it just runs in our family."* He was following in his dad's footsteps.

2. **Treasure Your Bible Dearly**

The second step is similar. **Not only must we love our Father deeply, we must treasure His Word dearly.**

5. Teach The Word Continually.

V. CONSECRATE

This word does not appear in the New Testament but is found 14 times in the Old Testament and each time it refers the subject listed.

1. Attendance (Time to the Lord)
2. Sharing our offering (Our means to the Lord)
3. Our Talents and gifts for the Lords use.

There are seven questions to ask yourself.

A. Am I consecrated to Him? Romans 12:1-2 tell us that we have to be consecrated before we can know the plan of God.

B. Am I spending time with Him? I find God's plan more and more as I spend more time with Him.

C. What are my gifts? Most of the time the plan of God fits right in with the gifts God has given us.

D. What are my desires? More often than not our desires and gifts fit together.

***E. What are my Christian friends saying*?** What do they say are my strengths and weaknesses?

F. What are my opportunities? What lies before me that God may be giving to me as an open door to walk through?

G. Am I in ministry now? It's amazing how many people who want to know God's plan for their lives are doing nothing now.

VI. CONTEMPLATE

Illustration: I love music of many tastes and remember a song the Jewish Barbara Streisand sang entitled, *"On a Clear day you can see forever."* While it is not a religious song it does present a truth we need to recognize. Because if we can see the end you will

1. See **sin** it its proper **prospective.**
2. You put the **Savior** in His **proper place**
3. You put **Service** in its **proper relationship.**

Illustration: A number of years ago, my wife and some traveling friends and me were in Vienna, Austria and noticed the ending of a Mozart symphony that night on a hotel placard. Later we flagged a taxi and headed to the concert hall.

The program was about to begin and I was intrigued as about 150 people had entered the stage in the dress of Mozart's era. White hair wigs and the garments of the period. The man in first chair of the violin section rose and step before the wind section and pulled his bow down and we began to hear those instruments sound their tune. Then he went before the string section and did the same and now the screeching from theirs. Finally, he approaches the remaining sections and now we have screech, boom, boom and toot, toot! It was disconcerting.

Next the conductor entered the stage and the first thing he did was shake hands with that violinist. I took a time to evaluate why he did this but later the answered was revealed to me.

Shortly, a group of six plays a tune together and each as they seated shook the man's hand in the first chair. Then two, or three or four played to us and each shook this man's had again.

During the next to the last song, the conductor left the room and again I wondered why.

While I sat there I notice every eye in the orchestra was looking at this man as he raised his bow and they started exactly at the same time as he came down the strings of his violin.

It was beautiful and I am now seeing it was this guy who was responsible to the training, teaching and practicing with the others. Then I said to myself they don't need the other guy. This guy does all the hard work!

Then the conductor returned, shook his hand again, and this final piece was outstandingly wonderful, and I left a convert to this music. Not the sound but the organization that made it great.

Let me make an application with this.

Our Lord Jesus has gone away and has left the work of training, teaching and outreach to the church. Our leadership is responsible for leading in these programs encouraging the fulfillment of the Lord's plan.

Then at His time, he will return, reward the church for its faithfulness.

I can already hear the last song, "All Hail the Power of Jesus Name. Let angel prostrate fall. Bring forth the diadem and crown Him lord of all."

www.ingramcontent.com/pod-product-compliance
Lightning Source LLC
Chambersburg PA
CBHW060919040426
42445CB00011B/701
* 9 7 8 1 9 4 0 6 0 9 2 9 4 *